RELIGIOUS CONFLICT IN AMERICA

Religious Conflict in America

STUDIES OF
THE PROBLEMS BEYOND BIGOTRY

Edited by Earl Raab

Anchor Books
Doubleday & Company, Inc.
Garden City, New York
1964

The abridgments of "Social Cleavage and Religious Conflict," by James S. Coleman (*The Journal of Social Issues,* Vol. XII, No. 3, 1956, pp. 44–56); and of *Protestant-Catholic-Jew,* by Will Herberg (New York: Doubleday & Company, Inc., 1955), appearing here under the title "The Religion of Americans and American Religion," are printed with the permission of the publishers and the approval of the authors. The edited selections from *The Religious Factor,* by Gerhard Lenski (New York: Doubleday & Company, Inc., 1961), appearing here under the title "The Four Socio-Religious Groups"; from "Interfaith Marriage: Problem or Symptom," by Clark E. Vincent in *Religion and the Face of America* (Berkeley, California: University Extension, University of California, 1958. Paper presented at Asilomar California conference in November 1958), appearing here under the title "Interfaith Marriages"; from "Religion and Politics in America," by Seymour Martin Lipset in Robert Lee, ed., *Religion and Social Conflict* (New York: Oxford University Press, forthcoming. Copyright © 1964 by Seymour Martin Lipset), appearing here under the title "Religion and Politics in American History"; from "Freedom and Separation: America's Contribution to Civilization," by Leo Pfeffer (*A Journal of Church and State,* Vol. II, No. 2, November 1960, pp. 100–11); from "Religion and Law in America," by Wilber G. Katz in Smith & Jamison, eds., *Religious Perspectives in American Culture* (Princeton: Princeton University Press, 1961. Copyright © 1961 by Princeton University Press. All rights reserved.), appearing here under the title "Freedom of Religion vs. Separation"; and from *Background Report* (New York: Project Religious Freedom and Public Affairs, National Conference of Christians and Jews, June 1962), appearing here under the title "Community Conflict: Christmas Observance in the Public School" are printed here by permission of the authors and publishers.

"Religious Responsibility for the Social Order: A Symposium by Three Theologians," by Jaroslav Pelikan, Gustave Weigel, and Emil L. Fackerheim (from papers presented at the 1962 annual meeting of the Project Religious Freedom and Public Affairs, National Conference of Christians and Jews in Washington, D.C.); "Religious Liberty from the Viewpoint of a Secular Humanist," by Sidney Hook (from "Religious Liberty from the Viewpoint of the Open Society," in *Cross Currents,* Winter Issue, 1963); and "America's Four Conspiracies," by John Courtney Murray (from *Religion in America,* John Cogley, ed., New York: Meridian Books, 1958. Copyright © 1958 by the Foundation for the Republic, Inc.) are reprinted here with permission of the publishers and the authors.

CONTENTS

THE NATURE OF THE CONFLICT: AN INTRODUCTION

There is reason to believe that interreligious conflict in America will finally prove to be a more knotty, more durable, and in some ways more significant problem than interracial conflict. It is certainly a more difficult problem to perceive. Religious bigotry is no longer the hard core of interreligious conflict, which has become bound to a series of related issues comprising "the religious conflict" in America. This religious conflict has indeed become sharper as religious bigotry has declined.

BACKGROUND OF BIGOTRY

There were periods in the seventeenth century when there was much more religious freedom in England than in the American colonies. In New England, Quakers were publicly whipped, branded, defaced, and hung. The various Protestant establishments generally oppressed and penalized deviant Protestant groups. Although less than one per cent of the American population was Catholic and most of these were in Maryland, anti-Catholic bias was also a standard part of the colonial culture. The raging Protestant-Catholic antagonism of Europe had been imported whole. Even in Maryland, after a surge of Protestant immigration, the colonial legislature in 1704 passed an act "to prevent the growth of popery." When Rhode Island, America's most tolerant colony, excluded Catholics from public office in 1719—a scant half century before the Revolution—there was no place where Catholics could practice their religion without disability. Much of the religious antagonism was, as always, rooted in national and political hostilities. But it was expressed as an antagonism of one religious creed towards another.

After the American Revolution, religious intolerance persisted in many vestigial forms. Official toleration under New Hampshire's laws was not granted to Baptists until 1804, not granted to Catholics until 1902. However, the national government, if not yet the states, was sharply enjoined at the outset from acts of religious intolerance. The emergence of the new nation coincided with the Age of Enlightenment, a high tide of religious and therefore interreligious indifferentism.

When interreligious conflict picked up its fevered history again, it was as an amalgam of old religious antagonisms and new social cleavages. About two million Irish Catholic immigrants arrived in this country between 1830 and 1860. Irish Catholics were attacked by mobs, their homes and churches burned to the ground. In 1844 the Catholic Bishop of Philadelphia was forced to close down the churches because of mob action.

However, the Irish Catholics were being attacked because they were Irish and immigrant, as well as because they were Catholic. The organized groups which led the attack, such as the Native American Party and the Know-Nothings, were essentially nativist and anti-immigrant in character.

During the Civil War, when half a million foreigners served in the Union forces, this new swell of anti-Catholicism subsided, only to rise again in the 1880s. During that decade over five million immigrants entered the country, large numbers of them Catholic Irish, joined by a growing stream of Catholic Italians as well as Jews from eastern Europe. This was a difficult period of economic adjustment for the country, culminating in the disastrous depression of 1893. The census of 1890 officially announced that the frontier was now "closed," that national expansion was at an end. The immigrants were visibly beginning to control big-city politics, the first Irish Catholic mayors having been elected in Boston, New York, and other cities in the 1880s. There were working-man resentments against immigration, agrarian resentments against the growing power of the cities, and general uneasiness about the folkways of these foreigners, all the more foreign because they were not Protestant. A host of anti-foreigner, anti-Catholic societies sprang up, including the reborn Ku Klux Klan and the American Protective Association, with some half million members in 1894. There was widespread discrimination against Catholic workers and Catholic businessmen. There were several major anti-Catholic riots in the 1890s. Anti-Catholic propaganda was in flood production. In Toledo, the mayor and the police commissioner bought rifles for the express purpose of repelling the Catholic invasion which they had been informed was in the making.

However, the anti-Catholicism of this period flowed more directly than ever from nativism, although traditional religious bigotry still colored it. Catholic churches were no longer in as much danger as individual Catholics, especially those of Irish and Italian descent. Interreligious conflict was severe, but it was now a unique American variety built essentially on non-religious grounds.

In some ways, anti-Catholicism was the anti-Semitism of nineteenth-century America. During most of the century, the Catholics were the religious group that bore the brunt of attack, discrimination, charges of conspiracy, political manipulation, and dual loyalty. Folk anti-Semitism was imported as part of the cultural baggage of English and European civilization, but it was non-virulent in early America. The Puritans had a certain affinity for the Hebrew civilization, and religious passions clashed on more active fronts.

At the time of the Revolution less than one tenth of one per cent of the population was Jewish. The proportions increased during the migrations of the early nineteenth century, and became substantial during the latter part of the century when Jews fled by the hundreds of thousands from eastern Europe. As foreigners, Jews also became targets for Protestant nativism. In the last two decades of the nineteenth century there occurred the country's first serious anti-Jewish violence. Jewish stores were wrecked in Louisiana, Jewish farm houses were burned in Mississippi, and when a glass works in New Jersey hired some Jews in 1891, there ensued several days of riots.

As in the case of the Catholics, the attacks against Jews were based not on religious grounds, but on other aspects of their group identity. They were useful as a fulcrum of social snobbery for the new moneyed classes, and social discrimination against Jews became a standard community institution throughout America along with related forms of economic discrimination. This kind of discrimination against Jews, especially in employment and housing, has declined demonstrably during the last two decades of the general "civil rights revolution."

But during the latter part of the nineteenth century, the Jews had also become a convenient political target for the anti-urban, anti-industrial discontents that accompanied social change in America. A strain of political anti-Semitism began to find expression in movements of agrarian unrest, as well as within the old established patrician society that was horrified by the new brawling industrial urban commercialism that seemed to be taking over the American way of life. For people like Henry Cabot Lodge and Henry Adams, the highly visible merchant Jews symbolized this new crass commercial spirit. Adams said in 1893 that "I have no place in a society of Jews and brokers."[1]

It was this thread of political anti-Semitism which came to full life in the 1920s and 1930s against the background of economic unrest and under the impact of a fully developed European ideology of anti-Semitism. The mainstream of anti-Semitism had become racism pure and simple. In the 1930s it is estimated that there were no less than 150 organizations promoting anti-Semitism in America, drawing inspiration and often more from the evangelistic racism of Nazi Germany.

Ideological and political anti-Semitism has tended to disappear from the American scene since the war against Nazi Germany, except for the furthest reaches of the political fringe. There is, of course, no way reliably to cal-

[1] Quoted by John Higham, "Anti-Semitism in the Gilded Age," *Mississippi Valley Historical Review*, March 1957.

culate the latent strength of this recurrent demonology. No one who watched the 1930s will be willing to guarantee that "it can't happen here." The folklore of anti-Semitism is still a standard part of the culture. But there is some reason to believe that ideological, political anti-Semitism has never been firmly grounded in American soil, and had its relative success in the earlier part of this century only as a backwash from Europe. In a sense, a native American anti-Catholicism pre-empted the field in the formative American years.

Meanwhile, this nativist anti-Catholicism had itself waned since the turn of the century. Discrimination against individual Catholics has largely disappeared. Myths about a "papal conspiracy" in America have lost currency. It became possible to elect a Catholic president partly because reflexive anti-Catholicism had become so attenuated. The questions that were raised about a Catholic candidate were indicative of the new order of concern. Typical was an Episcopal bishop who upheld the right of a Catholic candidate to be judged on his own individual merits; at the same time this Protestant churchman held that in order to determine the individual merits of a Catholic candidate, there was a *special* need to question him about his attitudes on church-state relationships.

The mainstream of interreligious hostility had moved from eighteenth-century religious grounds to nineteenth-century ethnic grounds, and finally to the mid-twentieth-century level of a debate on church-state issues. But these issues do not neatly arrange themselves along denominational lines; they are often only collaterally related to differences among religious groups.

CHURCH-STATE PROBLEMS

Defining the relationship between religion and human society is a generic problem; defining the relationship between church and state is a specialized aspect of that problem, resulting from the intervention of political rather than religious considerations. In America, the intervening political considerations are those of the modern democratic state and are suggested in two tantalizingly sparse clauses contained in the First Amendment to the Constitution.

The first clause directs Congress "to make no law respecting an establishment of religion." Behind this prescription lies the political concept of the "secular state."

The history of political states during a dozen centuries of Western Christian civilization had been a history of ecclesiastical rule and imperial rule "by divine origin." The concept of the modern democratic state was developed not only in revolt against older absolutist forms of powers, but in a period when philosophies of naturalism and rationalism were ascendant.

Jefferson wrote: "Reading, reflection and time have convinced me that the interests of society require observation of those moral principles only in which all religions agree . . . The practice of morality being necessary for the well-being of society, He (the Creator) has taken care to impress its precepts so indelibly on our hearts that they shall not be effaced by the subtleties of our brain."[2]

Not without its own subtleties, this statement suggests that God had already so sufficiently endowed man that any further intrusion of religious dogma would be not only unnecessary but harmful. The disposition of men's public affairs was to be left to men and to the rational faculties which they could bring to these affairs. Jefferson wrote that "truth is great and will prevail if left to herself (and unless) disarmed of her natural weapons, free argument and debate . . ."[3] Revelation and religious dogma were not subject to debate, and were therefore not to be directly imposed on the political process. The state was to be secular.

The second constitutional clause directs Congress to make no law "prohibiting the free exercise" of religion. This clause emphasizes the concept of religious liberty. Religious affiliation was to be voluntary, and religious con-

[2] H. A. Washington, editor, *Jefferson Writings*, New York, 1853–4, Vol. V, p. 471.

[3] Philip S. Foner, *Basic Writings of Thomas Jefferson* (Garden City, N.Y.: Halcyon House, 1944), p. 49.

science was not to be interfered with by the political state.

Together, these two clauses comprise the constitutional principle which has been called "separation of church and state." It has been said that Jefferson was interested in this principle in order to protect the state from religion, and that Roger Williams had been interested in the same principle in order to protect religion from the state. The two concerns may not be finally divisible. But it can similarly be said that the establishment clause approaches the "separation" principle by a stress on the inviolability of the secular state; the free-exercise clause approaches the "separation" principle by a stress on the inviolability of religious freedom. If a Catholic school child were somehow forced to participate in a Protestant religious exercise, the free-exercise clause could clearly be invoked. But even if all the children were willing and even if they were all of the same denomination, a religious exercise in the schools could run afoul of the establishment clause.

But the concepts of the secular state and of religious liberty are complicated by a third political principle of a more general nature: the state exists to serve the prevailing aspirations of the population at large, within the limitations prescribed by the Constitution. The question then becomes one of determining the precise limitations on majority will prescribed by the two relevant clauses of the First Amendment. In both cases, there are problems of interpretation.

The establishment clause reflects an inevitable tension between the concept of the secular state and the thrust of the American religious culture. No one has questioned that "separation" in this case certainly means separation between *church* and state. But to what extent is separation between *religion* and state required? At what point does an official religious invocation, reference, or exercise begin to seriously curb the secular nature of the state or hamper the Jeffersonian debate?

The free-exercise clause reflects an ongoing tension between the majority religious will and the individual religious conscience. At what point does government's accommodation to the prevailing religious culture violate the religious rights of deviant individuals?

There clearly is no absolute answer to either of these questions, and no blueprint that can be applied. The Supreme Court has said that this problem, "like many problems in constitutional law, is one of degree." Judge Learned Hand said that the canons of the First Amendment "are not jural concepts at all in the ordinary sense; and in application they turn out to be no more than admonitions of moderation."

There is, at the least, a constitutional *direction* in these admonitions. The old saw has it that a man is free to swing his fist up to the point of another man's nose—*not* that a man's nose has a right to be unbroken up to the point where it interferes with the swinging of another man's fist. At the least, the First Amendment prescription would hold that the religious culture can be expressed up to the point where the secular state is endangered; not that the secular state is to be maintained up to the point where it interferes with the prevailing religious culture. It would hold that the religious aspirations of the majority can be served up to the point where they interfere with the religious rights of an individual; not that the individual's religious rights are sacrosanct up to the point where they interfere with the religious aspirations of the majority. If a balance is to be struck between these tensions, it is to be struck within these directional limits.

Some hold that the only limits that are feasible are absolute limits which preclude any official state consideration of majority religious will or culture, and therefore eliminate the necessity of "balancing" these tensions at all. According to this view, the only safe way to safeguard the basic secular state and the religious rights of the individual is to operate a state which is stone blind to religion.

The practicality of such a course has been questioned, but further, it has been pointed out that the extension of such a "blindness" doctrine could finally serve to strip the majority of their "free exercise of religion." One of the functions of the democratic state, presumably, is to further the major aspirations of the population at large. If there is absolute separation of religion and state, beyond the limits required to guarantee a fundamentally secular state and the deviant religious conscience, then the majority's religious aspirations may be under certain circumstances unnecessarily curtailed. In 1962, when the U. S. Supreme Court found unconstitutional the recitation in public schools of a highly generalized prayer devised by the New York State Board of Regents on grounds that it violated the "establishment clause," one Justice dissented, saying: "I cannot see how an 'official religion' is established by letting those who want to say a prayer say it." The converse implication was that if the establishment clause was not being violated (and, of course, if no student was being forced to say the prayer), then the banishing of the prayer was a violation of the religious rights of those who did want to pray.

In other words, the tension between the secular state and the religious culture, as reflected in the establishment clause, was translated as a tension between the establishment clause and the free-exercise clause.

The Supreme Court has wrestled with these tensions and balances in a number of recent cases.

In two cases, the court ruled on "released-time" programs, whereby students who so desired were released from class an hour or two a week to attend religious classes under the auspices of their own church or synagogue. In 1948, the court ruled that such programs were unconstitutional when held on school grounds. In 1952, the court found that such programs were constitutional when held off of school grounds, since they only "accommodated to religious needs," even though some administrative assistance from the school system was involved. In 1962, the court ruled that the New York State Regents prayer was unconstitutional, even though students could be exempted upon request. In 1963, the court found that Bible-reading and the recitation of the Lord's Prayer in the schools were also unconstitutional.

These Supreme Court decisions have typically created a ferment of national excitement; indeed a ferment which the specific practices involved in these cases have not clearly warranted. Released-time programs provide an hour or two of "weekday Sunday school" to that small band—perhaps 5 per cent—of America's schoolchildren who elect it. Many communities have discontinued the program because of slim attendance. One prominent Protestant theologian, Reinhold Niebuhr, objected strenuously to the court's prohibition of the New York Regents prayer, but acknowledged: "I do not think religion in our culture will stand or fall by the presence or absence of the Regent's prayer . . ."[4] Bible-reading would also seem to be included in the admonition of another Protestant author, Edwin O. Miller, that "meaningful prayer takes place within an appropriate context, not as classroom routine along with the salute to the flag."[5] There is much evidence that biblical recitation or knowledge, by itself, without a deeper religious discussion and commitment, has limited religious effect. However, religious tokenism is a dull knife that cuts neither way. If religion is not seriously advanced by such shallow exercises, then neither is the secular state nor the deviant individual conscience seriously threatened by them.

There is always, of course, the "principle of the thing." If the integrity of a principle is violated under any circumstances, it is presumably weakened for all circumstances. It is the business of the Supreme Court to clarify these principles for their own sake. But the kind of public asperity which has surrounded these cases suggests that there is more at stake than an abstract debate on church-state relations. The legalistic welter tends to hide the fact that church-state questions, in addition to having their own intrinsic importance, are surrogates for more comprehensive issues actively stirring in American society: one reflecting a basic tension in America's political life; the other reflecting a basic tension in America's religious life.

[4] Quoted in "Religious Reactions to the Regent's Prayer Decision," *Interreligious Newsletter*, New York: Anti-Defamation League.
[5] Ibid.

THE POLITICAL ISSUE:
POPULISM VS. CONSTITUTIONALISM

That aspect of the church-state debate which emphasizes majority will vs. minority rights reflects a recurrent and often critical tug between populist impulses and constitutional limitations. As defined generically by Edward A. Shils, "populism proclaims that the will of the people as such is supreme over every other standard, over the standards of traditional institutions, over the autonomy of institutions and over the will of other strata. Populism identifies the will of the people with justice and morality."[6] At its most extreme, populism can be used to simulate and pervert the democratic concept, as it has typically done in modern totalitarian societies. At its best, the populist tendency is a check against the use of constitutional forms to prevent social change. Populism is a highly volatile but necessary ingredient in modern social revolutions.

The American Revolution, more legal than social, did not start with a burst of populism, but the populist tendency has been a constant strand in American history. It has often been the case that widespread discontent has manifested itself in impatience with constitutional procedures. The Supreme Court as a final arbiter of constitutional limitations has frequently been the symbolic target of these frustrations. In the depth of the Great Depression, when the Supreme Court was ruling out a number of the economic measures of the New Deal, there was a strong populist move to evade the court by "packing it" with additional members.

Many of the current changes in American society and in the world have created some apparently insoluble problems and new veins of discontent and frustration, e.g.: The knotty interracial problems of both the North and the South, America's cramped style on the new international

[6] Edward A. Shils, *The Torment of Secrecy* (Glencoe, Illinois: The Free Press, 1956), p. 98.

scene. More generally, from these and other problems related to the cities, the youth, and the economy, there has developed a widespread feeling that traditional controls are somehow irretrievably slipping away.

These frustrations have often drawn taut the natural tension between populist and constitutional tendencies in American life. Some of this tension has been conveniently displaced on church-state questions.

Southern legislators, still restive under the 1954 decision of the court ordering desegregation of the schools, were markedly vehement in their denunciation of the New York Regents prayer decision in 1962. "They put the Negroes in the schools and now they've driven God out of them," commented one representative from Alabama.[7] A senator from Georgia said: "For some years now the members of the Supreme Court have persisted in reading alien meanings into the Constitution. . . ."[8] A senator from Mississippi used the occasion to sponsor an amendment to the Constitution which would allow each state substantially to by-pass the Constitution in its enactment of legislation "based on its own public policy based on decency and morality."[9]

Other legislators had been frustrated by limitations which the court had placed on some subversive-control legislation. The chairman of the House Unamerican Activities Committee said about the New York Regents Prayer decision: "This is just one more decision in line with the philosophy guiding the group of men sitting there as justices of our court of last resort."[10] Among the thousands of organizational and individual expressions of dissatisfaction with the 1962 and 1963 Supreme Court decisions, there was a constant repetition of this theme as expressed in one

[7] Representative George Andrews, quoted in the New York *Herald Tribune,* June 26, 1962.

[8] Senator Henry Talmadge quoted in "The Supreme Court and the Regents' Prayer, The Dialogue" (New York: National Conference of Christians and Jews, 1962).

[9] Senator James O. Eastland, ibid.

[10] Representative Francis E. Walter, ibid.

public letter: "Don't the wishes of the majority in this country mean anything anymore?"[11]

THE RELIGIOUS ISSUE: THE SEARCH FOR VALUES

Religion, as traditionally conceived, was at low ebb at the country's birth. "The new nation," writes one church historian, "was a heathen nation."[12] It is estimated that in 1776 only about 5 per cent of the American people were church members. The churches were able to exert little influence. The mass of people were, at the least, religiously indifferent. Many of the Revolution's leaders and intellectuals, the Founding Fathers, were guilty of the "French infidelity"; an explicit rejection of revealed religion in favor of deism. None of the first four presidents of the United States belonged to a traditional church. George Washington, Thomas Jefferson, John Adams, and James Madison, as well as many other early American leaders were either deists or Unitarians.

The Constitutional Convention of 1777 made passing mention only of the "Great Governor of the World." The Declaration of Independence included such phrases as "the Supreme Judge of the World" and "Divine Providence." Thomas C. Hall commented that such documents were "as completely secular as the by-laws of an insurance company."[13] Thomas Paine expressed a widespread intellectual sentiment when he found "an adequate revelation of God in the constitution of nature." In his very first general order, George Washington instructed each of his men to "live and act as becomes a Christian soldier," but

[11] From Letters to the Editor, New York *Daily News*, June 29, 1962.
[12] This theme runs through Franklin Hamlin Littell, *From State Church to Pluralism* (Garden City: Doubleday Anchor Books, 1962).
[13] Thomas C. Hall, *The Religious Background of American Culture* (New York: Frederick Ungar Publishing Co., 1930), p. 169.

his context was a Christian civilization rather than a formal Christian religion. Insofar as the concepts of morality and God were separated from any commitment to revelation or theology, the "religion" that remained was by definition secularized.

Secularism is not, of course, a synonym for atheism. The term "secular" itself merely describes those aspects of man's life which are "of the world," finite, civil, non-ecclesiastical. Secularism denotes the relative ascendancy of secular institutions over religious institutions, or, the ascendancy of secular considerations over sacred considerations. Even at its more aggressive, secularism does not necessarily deny the existence of God, although it does tend to hold that man rather than God is the measure of social behavior.

In fact, religious tendencies and secularist tendencies have flourished side by side in America. By 1850, more than 15 per cent of the American people were church-affiliated; by 1900 more than a third of the American people were affiliated. By 1963, when there seemed to be a "leveling off," two thirds of the nation were affiliated. History had never recorded such a spectacular religious growth. The United States now led the world in voluntary church membership.

But religious life had changed character as it grew. The growth had been characterized in the nineteenth century by a series of great revival movements which swept the country. These were missionary movements, in effect, and addressed in large part to America's rapidly moving frontiers. But they were also shaped by the nature and needs of these frontiers. Traditional forms of organization, ritual, and theological dogma were de-emphasized. Personal religious experience was emphasized. The over-all effect of this frontier experience was to generalize the mainstream of American religion. Religious complexities gave way to common denominators.

Traditional religious doctrine was further eroded by a latter-day mood of naturalism, pragmatism, and secular optimism which accompanied the phenomenal growth of science, industry, and wealth. One American theologian

said: "The new theology seeks to recover spiritual processes from the magical to a moral conception."[14] Another
said: "A valid Christianity is to be known not by its roots
but by its fruits."[15]

Religion had become part of the American Way of Life,
its institutions and rhetoric flourished, but it had itself become secularized. Religion was now often primarily measured by its ability to contribute to the strength of secular
life, to democracy, to social well-being. The relationship
between man's religious beliefs and his social behavior had
been reversed, or at the least, severed in a new version
of the French Infidelity.

In various polls, about 96 per cent of the American
people say they believe in God, but about 80 per cent
indicate that they are more concerned about a comfortable
life on earth rather than about any other-worldly considerations, and 54 per cent admit that their religious beliefs do not have any effect on the way they conduct their
daily business. Gerhard Lenski's study of religious life in
Detroit concluded that at least among Protestants, "despite attending the churches more frequently, their
thoughts and values are less often derived from distinctly
religious sources and more often derived from secular
sources."[16]

Religious leaders worry about the disparity between religious affiliation and religious commitment. They also
worry about an American society without religious commitment. According to Rabbi Abraham Joshua Heschel:
"The central problem of this generation is emptiness in
the heart, the decreased sensitivity to the imponderable
quality of the spirit, the collapse of communication between the realm of tradition and the inner world of the
individual."[17]

[14] From Theodore Munger, *Essays For the Day* (Boston:
Houghton Mifflin, 1904), p. 7.
[15] Charles D. Williams, *A Valid Christianity for Today*
(New York: Macmillan Co., 1909), pp. VII–VIII.
[16] See Gerhard Lenski, "The Four Socio-Religious Groups."
[17] Abraham Joshua Heschel, "The Religious Message," in
Religion in America, John Cogley, ed. (New York: Meridian,
1958), p. 256.

Many theologians warn that secular moral habits and humanistic values do not automatically replenish themselves and that "the faith upon which these values were based no longer animate many of those who profess the values. . . . [The values] depend for their propulsion upon sources of power beyond themselves and beyond their own culture."[18]

But there is more involved than a religious-secular tension about sources of value. As American society seems to linger in a kind of limbo between its past and its future, there is a tension between the old and the new. The sociologists worry about the "value-vacuum" in an America in limbo, and point to a rise in a variety of social and personal pathologies. This sense of a loss of values is expressed in less theoretical terms by various sections of the population, many of whom see the religious tradition of America, however secularized it may have become, as symbolic of America's past, of values lost. And there is no doubt that America's history is intertwined with religious tradition and rhetoric.

President Eisenhower said: "You cannot otherwise explain our government except on the basis of a deeply felt religious faith." And the U. S. Supreme Court has held that "we are a religious people whose institutions presuppose a Supreme Being." There is surely built into the American culture a pervasive "faith in faith," an affinity for religious traditions and institutions.

There are then two levels of conflict: a genuine religious-secular tension and a simulated religious-secular tension, really a tug between traditional America as identified by its religion-culture, and a plastic new America. These concerns and tensions have clearly intruded themselves into the debate on church-state issues.

Evangelist Billy Graham stated about the 1962 Supreme Court decision: "The decision is another step towards secularism . . ."[19] Cardinal Spellman called it another ex-

[18] See Jaroslav Pelikan, "Religious Responsibility For the Social Order."
[19] New York *Herald Tribune*, June 28, 1962.

ample of the secularists' aim "to strip America of all her religious tradition."[20] In Pittsburgh the Episcopal bishop and the Catholic bishop issued a joint statement attacking the "powerful, aggressive spirit of secularism." And one Protestant theologian who acknowledged that the Regents Prayer was not of much religious value in itself was nevertheless concerned with it as "a symbol of the religious life and tradition of the nation."[21]

These are, to some degree, irrelevant intrusions. The principle of the secular state, for example, is itself essentially a political principle, neither religious nor irreligious. But "church-state questions," under the pressure of these other tensions in American life, cannot be understood or perhaps dealt with forever in a legalistic vacuum. If "balances" are to be struck, they will be struck under these pressures. Nor are the constitutional limitations themselves immutable.

MODERN INTERRELIGIOUS CONFLICT

Neither the church-state issues in their purity nor the issues which are imposed upon them result directly from religious group differences. All of these issues cut somewhat across denominational lines. However, many religious group differences do relate to these issues, and result finally in an intergroup conflict about the issues themselves. This intergroup conflict adds another religion-connected issue to American life: the viability of religious pluralism.

Actually there are few differences of religious dogma which directly became a subject of public dissension. For the most part, the imperatives of public morality deriving from American Christianity, Judaism, and secular humanism have become a common stream. There have been a few exceptions, notably the theologically based antagonism of many Protestant groups to gambling and liquor; and the Catholic religious strictures against divorce and artificial birth control. Some strains have been placed on

[20] Ibid.
[21] Reinhold Niebuhr, *Interreligious Newsletter*, July 9, 1962.

many of America's pluralistic communities as a result of these differences in themselves.

More pervasive in effect, however, have been the differences in religious character which have affected disparate church needs. There are differences in corporate emphasis, in emphasis on the primal importance of the historical religious body itself. There is usually an accompanying dependence on ritual procedures and institutions. Catholicism is relatively high on this index; Protestantism, with its historical concentration on the religious individual, relatively low. There is, of course, wide variation among Protestant denominations, as there is among the denominations of Judaism, which historically has a strong corporate emphasis of its own.

Father Edward Duff explains why a Catholic might be more dismayed than, say, a Baptist by the removal of the chaplains from the Armed Forces:

> A Baptist boy can presumably open his Bible in the barracks, and inspired by the revelation it contains, satisfy his essential religious needs. Not so the Catholic. Draft him for a part of his life where he is deprived of access to a priest, an instrument he believes irreplaceable to forgive his sins and to give him the Bread of Life, and you have egregiously, if thoughtlessly, trampled on his religious freedom . . . Moreover, authoritative teaching is of (Catholicism's) essence.[22]

Its corporate emphasis on institution, and on "authoritative teaching," plus its position in American life, led the Catholic Church to develop a massive network of private religious schools, which has always been a center of public controversy. Over five million children attend church-connected elementary or secondary schools rather than public schools. Over 90 per cent of these are Catholic children attending Catholic schools. This is a matter of institutional orientation and investment, rather than of

[22] Father Edward Duff, S.J., "A Catholic Looks at Religious Liberty," *Cross Currents*, Winter 1963, p. 56.

specific religious dogma. Well over half of all American Catholic schoolchildren attend public schools.

The obvious dilemma for Catholics has been that religious instruction in America's public schools was always bound to have a Protestant cast, and the absence of religious instruction left an intolerable institutional gap. The same dilemma has existed for the Orthodox Jewish community, which has a proportionately high enrollment in religious all-day schools.

Recent proposals for providing federal financial aid to local public schools have been accompanied by Catholic claims that church-connected schools should also benefit from such aid, since the religious schools provide the state-prescribed secular education as well.

This specific issue has lent special passion to some ostensibly unrelated church-state issues. After the Supreme Court decision on the New York Regents Prayer, one official Baptist statement said that the bitter response of the Catholic hierarchy was really related to their concern for federal aid to parochial schools. The Annual Assembly of the Christian Churches approved the Supreme Court ruling, saying that "this ruling precludes a later favorable ruling breaking down separation of church and state in relation to public support for parochial schools."[23]

There are differences also in emphasis on doctrinal orthodoxy, on the singleness of religious truth. Catholicism is again higher on this index than the mainstream of modern Protestantism, but no higher than many segments of fundamentalist Protestantism. However, the nub of the public issue is not religious orthodoxy per se, but the extension of that orthodoxy to the political scene.

In 1962, for example, Virginia passed a law permitting physicians to sterilize patients over twenty-one who requested the operation. Archbishop O'Boyle of Washington attacked the law in these words:

Sterilization of individuals, whether voluntary or compulsory is fundamentally wrong not only because the Catholic Church says it is wrong but because it

[23] *Interreligious Newsletter*, Vol. VII, No. 1, February 1963.

directly violates a natural right which is so profoundly sacred that it may not be taken away from the individual by the State and may not be voluntarily surrendered to the State by the individual.[24]

Many Protestant ministers immediately disagreed, including a Unitarian minister in Washington who called the law morally "good," and asked:

Does sterilization violate God's law? It violates what the Roman Catholic Church believes God's law to be. But is this God's law? Who shall say? Who but men? And to which men shall we grant the right to tell us what God's law is? What's the natural law but what men say it is?[25]

There is evident in this exchange more than a simple incompatibility of religious viewpoint on the matter of sterilization. There is also evident a comprehensive concern about the operation of a non-empirical "natural law" in the public sphere. This finally returns to the hard-core issue of the integrity of the secular state: the fear that if some religious groups acquire political power, directly or indirectly, they would feel religiously compelled to impose their social imperatives on everyone else.

This fear of religious power over the state is most often expressed as a fear of Catholic power. It is not that Protestantism has been above imposing some of its dogmatic points by means of political power. But Protestantism is fragmented, and is neither as ideologically geared to nor as historically identified with the specter of church domination as is Catholicism.

Those who raise this specter are likely to quote statements such as this one by the world Jesuit journal in 1945:

The Roman Catholic Church, convinced through its divine prerogatives of being the only true church, must demand the right of freedom for herself alone,

[24] Gerald Grant, "The Fauquier Hospital Sterilization Story," *Background Reports* (New York: National Conference of Christians and Jews, January 1963), pp. 4 and 5.
[25] Ibid.

because such a right can only be possessed by truth, never by error. As to other religions, the church will certainly never draw the sword, but she will require that by legitimate means they shall never be allowed to propagate false doctrine. Consequently, in a state where the majority of people are Catholic, the Church will require that legal existence be denied to error.[26]

But there was also this affirmation in 1960 by a group of leading American Catholic laymen "in the freedom of the religious conscience and the Catholic's obligation to guarantee full freedom of belief and worship as a civil right . . . we deplore the denial of religious freedom in any land. We especially deplore this denial in countries where Catholics constitute a majority—even an overwhelming majority."[27]

Beyond matching quotations however, it is necessary to take into account the quickening response of the Catholic Church to the modern world, as dramatized by the historic leadership of Pope John XXIII, e.g.: the increase in biblical criticism, the inexorable movement towards greater autonomy by local bishops and towards more decisive lay participation in the affairs of the Church; the explicit recognition of the needs of the modern democratic state.

It is also necessary to take into account the overriding social and political characteristics of the Catholic laity in America, where, for example, a substantial proportion of middle-class Catholics do practice one form or another of artificial birth control; and where there is a prevalent cultural commitment to the fundamental concepts of church-state separation.

Much of the fear of "Catholic power" is mechanistically rooted in the past, and is clearly exaggerated. However, there *are* significant religious differences, in character, in institutional need, and even in dogma which tend to set Catholics off from non-Catholics.

---

[26] *Civilta Cattolica*, Rome, April 1945, as quoted in Leo Pfeffer, *Creeds in Competition* (New York: Harper, 1958), p. 37.
[27] *Catholic Mind*, March–April 1961, p. 179.

STATUS DIFFERENCES

The Jewish community has a good historical reason for being jealous of the prerogatives of the secular state. Until the rise of the secular state, they had never known religious freedom in the West. As a permanent religious minority, they are uneasy about any relaxation of the constitutional admonitions on church-state relations. As an ethnic minority, with special historical memories, they are concerned with any apparent erosion of constitutional limitations. As a cultural minority in the midst of a third-generation quest for continuity, they are wary about being smothered by the Christian culture around them.

A special sensitivity to church-state matters was also characteristic of the American Catholic community during the nineteenth and early twentieth centuries. The first challenge to Bible-reading in the schools was made by Catholic parents in Maine in 1854. Between 1872 and 1905, Catholic parents in seven other states instituted actions on similar grounds. At one point early in its history the Catholic community retreated from its request for public aid to Catholic schools in the face of vehement reaction. Today, the Catholic community no longer hesitates to make its request on that account. Catholics are emerging from their posture as a "defensive minority." Indeed, their status as a minority is questionable. There are over forty million Catholics in the country. While there are more than sixty million Protestants, the largest single Protestant church organization is the Methodist Church with something over ten million members. No precise comparison is possible between membership figures in Protestant churches and the Catholic Church because the latter regards all baptized persons, including children, as members—but the fact must still remain that Catholicism is the largest single denomination in the country. The influence of the Catholic community is all the more potent because of its concentration in the large and politically important population centers. And today there is an impelling intellectual and organizational ferment in the Catholic community. Catholic defensiveness has given way to a confident outward thrust into the life of the community.

It is Protestantism which has become more defensive, and not just out of a concern with the growing vigor of Catholicism. There is a sense that America is, for other reasons, witnessing the "end of the Protestant era." Certainly at an end is the century during which the political life of the country was dominated by the Protestant Midwest. At an end is the "way of life" developed in Protestant rural America. Protestant churches are still attempting to adapt themselves to the problems and patterns of the big cities, in which they have always been weakest. Over much of the Protestant community, there hangs a special sense of draining power and loss of traditional values. There are newly aggressive Protestant churches and theologians, seeking new denominational alliances, launching urban social action programs, and evincing a positive concern with the "secularization" of American Protestant culture. There are also strains of brooding over the past, which tend to encourage religious fundamentalism and give impetus to movements of political discontent and populism.

RELIGIOUS SEPARATISM

There is an apparent riddle in the fact that religion in America has moved in a generalized direction, while at the same time certain kinds of interdenominational conflict have flourished.

The vast majority of the American population has strong denominational loyalties, at least as Protestants, Catholics, or Jews. According to one survey only about 5 per cent of these Americans who identify themselves with one of these major denominations were "born into" a different denomination. But their loyalties are based on cultural, institutional, social, and historical ties, as well as on theological ties. There has been much research evidence, for example, that ethnic intermarriage has far outpaced religious intermarriage. This resistance to religious exogamy is presumably related to but not dependent on the existence of strong socioeconomic differences among the various religious faiths. There are also obvious cultural, ethnic, and geographical differences. And there is the simple fact that, for the church-affiliated, social associations tend to arrange themselves around church-connected activities.

The evidence suggests that, very broadly speaking, theological commitment is often a less salient factor in religious identification than commitment to the religious group itself, and to the religious institution which embraces the group. The theological considerations underlying many of the differences in religious group need and character exist at the institutional level. Because of these interlocking social and creedal patterns, it is likely that certain aspects of religious group separatism in America will outlast racial separatism. Many of these religious group differences are, after all, properly "beyond social remedy."

SUMMARY

Religious conflict in America today is not only not what it was, it is usually not quite what it seems to be. The bundle of religion-connected tensions which comprise "the religious conflict" is not primarily produced by interreligious differences, nor by controversy about church-state relationships. Its often hidden source is America's growing panic over a lost past and what seems to be a crumbling value base.

Church-state issues are hypothetically independent exercises in the definition of America's political nature with respect to secular state and religious liberty. These are primarily political issues, not religious issues. But various religion-connected issues typically—and often irrelevantly—penetrate the public debate. The church-state debate, therefore, is itself not finally irrelevant to the larger issues which intrude upon it.

Interreligious issues are hypothetically independent exercises in pluralism, based on differences among religious groups in dogma and institutional character. But these interreligious differences confront each other mainly on the battleground of church-state issues.

The various interreligious differences increasingly manifest themselves as church-state questions for the same kinds of reasons that the religious-secular tension and the uneasiness about religion-connected traditions so often show up as church-state questions. The state's presence is felt in vastly widening areas of private life. In the past generation, the average number of student-hours per school-age population has doubled. The extension of governmental welfare institutions into private life has been even more spectacular. Regulations and subventions have multiplied. It is difficult to venture very far in any major social activity, whether it be birth control programs or education, without encountering some presence of the state.

Concomitantly, the concept of the neutral state, the state which exists primarily to adjudicate and protect, has largely disappeared. The state is now perceived as the proper agency and perhaps the only agency through which many of the needs and aspirations of the people can be actively aided and supported. If there is any phenomenon which needs buttressing, from institutions to symbolic traditions, it has become more and more likely that aid will be sought from the government.

Church-state issues have consequently become a likely arena for the confrontation of interreligious differences, as well as for other religion-connected tensions. It is not that there are really critical differences among the various religious groups today as to basic church-state principles themselves. There is a general consensus as to the fundamental concepts of religious liberty, and even of the secular state. But the differences in religious character, in institutional needs, in history, and in status create different stresses on these principles, and different interpretations of the kinds of balances which should be struck within them. The Catholic community, for example, tends to emphasize the need for government aid and accommodation to religious institutions. The Protestant community tends to emphasize government support for the traditional religion-culture and is in many cases extremely resistant to proposals for institutional aid. The Jewish community tends to emphasize the constitutional limitations themselves. These and other differences in stance, resulting from different religious needs and different religious group needs, pose problems in pluralistic accommodation. But there is even more at issue than pluralism, or interreligious harmony or the nature of the secular state and religious liberty. Embroiled in these issues, and often tested by them, are larger definitions of America's political and religious nature, e.g.: the nature of our constitutional government, the nature of our religious life, the source and cogency of our national values.

In short, the total bundle of religion-connected issues presses into any single issue and invests it with an acrimony and a significance which it would not otherwise have. For intergroup relations, as well as for the democratic dialogue in general, there is posed a stunningly sophisticated problem in the communication and negotiation of differences. The dialogue breaks down unless the participants are discussing the same issue at the same time, which is infrequently the case; and unless the participants are able to consider simultaneously all of the correlative issues, without confusing one with the other. It is because of this continuing difficulty that one observer has written that "the conflict, as one sees it developing slowly but surely before our eyes, bodes ill for our society. The situation is one that calls for heart-searching and the highest reaches of statesmanship."[28]

The selections in this volume move generally from a treatment of various aspects of interreligious differences and conflicts, to the matter of the religious-secular conflict in America, to a discussion of the church-state issue

[28] Milton Konvitz, *Congress Weekly*, March 3, 1952, as quoted in Will Herberg, "The Sectarian Conflict Over Church and State," *Commentary*, Vol. 14, No. 5, November 1952, p. 462.

which so often serves as a vehicle for other elements of the religious conflict.

Gerhard Lenski ("The Four Socio-Religious Groups") describes what one study has revealed about the social and religious differences among major religious groups in one American city.

Clark E. Vincent ("Interfaith Marriages") summarizes and comments on the knowledge that is available about one ultimate index of interreligious separatism: intermarriage.

Seymour Martin Lipset ("Religion and Politics in American History") analyzes the manner in which interreligious differences have affected and have been manifested through a specific phenomenon in American life: its politics.

James S. Coleman ("Social Cleavage and Religious Conflict") proposes a theoretical framework within which the various aspects of religious conflict might be understood.

Will Herberg ("The Religion of Americans and American Religion") describes the basic nature and development of the religious-secular conflict in America, and suggests some of its implications.

Jaroslav Pelikan, Gustave Weigel, and *Emil L. Fackenheim* ("Religious Responsibility for the Social Order: a Symposium") approach the problem of relating the religious and secular elements in our society from the vantage points, respectively, of a Protestant, Catholic, and Jewish theologian.

Sidney Hook ("Religious Liberty from the Viewpoint of a Secular Humanist") approaches the same problem from the vantage point of a secular humanist.

Leo Pfeffer ("Freedom and Separation") deals with the specific issue of church-state relations as an advocate of a strict interpretation of the principle of church-state separation.

Wilber Katz ("Freedom of Religion Versus Separation") deals with the same issue as an advocate of a more flexible interpretation of the principle of church-state separation.

The U. S. Supreme Court ("The Supreme Court on

Church and State") makes its own comments by way of pertinent excerpts from recent opinions.

"Community Conflict" is a journalistic case study of the tensions that developed in one city around a specific church-state issue, on which was superimposed a number of other elements of the religious conflict.

John Courtney Murray ("America's Four Conspiracies") reviews the total religious conflict in America and suggests the kind of democratic and interreligious dialogue which that conflict is going to require.

THE FOUR SOCIO-RELIGIOUS GROUPS

Gerhard Lenski

The purpose of this study is to discover what *difference* religion actually makes in the everyday life of the citizen. The findings are based on interviews with 656 selected Detroiters in 1958. Strictly speaking, therefore, the findings apply only to Detroit. However, in view of the steady decline of localism and regionalism in America during the last century, it seems likely that most of these findings could be duplicated by similar studies in most other metropolitan centers.

The four major socio-religious groups in Detroit are white Protestants (41 per cent), white Catholics (35 per cent), Negro Protestants (15 per cent), and Jews (4 per cent). The remaining 5 per cent of the population is made up of persons with no religious preference, and of Eastern Orthodox, Negro Catholics, and a very small number of Moslems and Buddhists.

It was necessary to distinguish between two aspects of membership in a religious group. A religious group is not just a formal association based on religious ties. There are also a vast number of highly personal and very basic relationships—such as those between friends or between the members of a family—which constitute an integral part of every religious group. In short, religious groups are communal as well as associational groups. Hence the analysis must take account of religious communities, or subcommunities, as well as formal religious associations.

I. STRENGTH OF GROUP TIES

The pattern at present

When one examines the four major socio-religious groups in Detroit in the light of our distinction between the association and the subcommunity, it quickly becomes evident that each is a distinctive type of social organization. The Jewish and Catholic groups present the sharpest contrasts, so let us examine them first.

THE JEWISH GROUP

In the case of Judaism we are confronted with a group in which the religious associations have been seriously weakened. In a recent analysis of church attendance in the Detroit area by Harold Orbach, it was found that only 12 per cent of the Jews reported regular weekly attendance at synagogue or temple.[1] Another 20 per cent reported attending at least once a month, and 56 per cent only on High Holy Days, or a few times a year. Twelve per cent did not attend at all.

On the basis of such evidence one might conclude that the ties binding the individual to the group are very weak. However, the 1958 survey indicates that while the *associational* bond is weak in the Jewish group, the *communal* bond is extremely strong. In fact, available evidence indicates that the communal bond in the Jewish group is as strong, or stronger, than in any other group. For example, it was found that all of the Jewish respondents in our sample who were married were lifelong Jews married to a lifelong Jewish spouse.[2] When asked what proportion of

---

[1] Harold L. Orbach, "Aging and Religion," *Geriatrics*, 16, October 1961, pp. 530–40. This approach may well underrate the strength of associational ties among Jews, since in the original design of this study, there was insufficient recognition of the number and strength of *secular* Jewish associations.

[2] In the special sample survey of 1957 the Bureau of the Census included a question on religious preference. One of the findings of this census was that over 96 per cent of all American

their close relatives were Jewish, 96 per cent said that all or nearly all were Jewish. When asked the same question about their close friends, 77 per cent reported that all or nearly all were Jewish. Such evidence makes it clear that while the ties binding individual Jews to their religious associations have been seriously weakened in modern times, the ties of communalism remain strong. If our sample is at all reliable, the great majority of Detroit Jews find most of their primary relationships within the Jewish subcommunity.

THE CATHOLIC GROUP

The white Catholic group presents a very different picture in every respect. On the basis of Orbach's six-year survey, it appears that more than 70 per cent of Detroit Catholics attend Mass at least once a week and only about 5 per cent fail to attend at all. While there may be some measure of exaggeration in these figures, it is certain that the ties binding the individual to the nuclear association are far stronger in Catholicism than in Judaism.

In the case of communal ties, the situation is exactly reversed. Catholics are far more inclined than Jews to marry and establish other intimate personal relationships outside their group. Sixteen per cent of the Catholic respondents in the 1958 survey reported that they were currently married to non-Catholics. In addition still others had contracted marriages with non-Catholics who ultimately became Catholics, or themselves left the Catholic Church as a consequence of marrying non-Catholics, so that 30 per cent of all those who were raised as Catholics married someone who was raised a non-Catholic.

In view of the high rate of intermarriage between Cath-

Jews are married to persons currently professing to be Jews. For Catholics the comparable figure was 89 per cent. For all Protestants, both Negro and white, the figure was nearly 96 per cent. In interpreting these figures it must be kept in mind that Protestants are much more likely to marry Protestants merely because of chance, since 66 per cent of all Americans aged fourteen and over are Protestants, while this is much less likely for Catholics and Jews, who constitute only 26 and 3 per cent of the population respectively.

olics and non-Catholics, it is hardly surprising that a substantial minority of Catholics have a significant number of close relatives who are non-Catholics. Whereas 96 per cent of the Jews reported that all or nearly all of their close relatives were Jewish, only 79 per cent of the Catholics reported that all or nearly all of their close relatives were Catholics. There was an even more pronounced discrepancy with respect to ties of friendship. Whereas 77 per cent of the Jewish respondents reported that all or nearly all of their close friends were Jewish, the comparable figure for Catholics was only 44 per cent.

On the basis of such data we can see that Judaism and Catholicism represent two distinct types of socio-religious groups in the modern metropolis. In the Jewish group communal ties predominate, and ties with religious associations are extremely weak. In the Catholic group the relationship is reversed, though it would be an exaggeration to say that Catholic communal ties are weak.

THE WHITE PROTESTANT GROUP

In the white Protestant group still another pattern emerges. The proportion of white Protestants who attend worship services regularly falls far below the Catholic figure, though not nearly so low as in the Jewish group. In Orbach's six-year survey it was found that roughly one third of the white Protestants in Detroit attend worship services every Sunday. Slightly more than 20 per cent attend from one to three times a month, and 14 per cent never attend. The remaining third attend occasionally.

In communal solidarity and strength, however, white Protestants closely match white Catholics. Whereas 84 per cent of the white Catholics who were married reported that their spouses were of the same faith, 86 per cent of the white Protestants made the same statement. Whereas 70 per cent of those who were raised Catholics married someone raised a Catholic, 73 per cent of the white Protestants married someone raised a Protestant. Seventy-nine per cent of the white Catholics and 76 per cent of the white Protestants reported that all or nearly all of their close relatives were of the same faith. Finally, 44 per cent of the white Catholics reported that all or nearly all of their close friends were of the same faith; the corresponding figure for white Protestants was 38 per cent.

Judging from such evidence, it appears that the white Protestant group is the least cohesive of the three white socio-religious groups. It lacks the very strong communal bond of the Jewish group, and it lacks the very strong associational bond of the Catholic group. In terms of the *relative* strength of these two bonds, however, the white Protestant group resembles the Jewish group a bit more than the Catholic group since the communal bond seems to be somewhat stronger than the associational bond. However, this resemblance should not be exaggerated; the differences are still very real.

THE NEGRO PROTESTANT GROUP

In the Negro Protestant group the communal bond is extremely strong, owing to the discriminatory practices of whites. In the realm of primary relationships—intimate relations of kinship and friendship—segregation tends to be the rule in the urban North almost as much as in the rural South. Of necessity, therefore, the overwhelming majority of Negroes in Detroit marry other Negroes, and find their intimate personal relationships with others of their own race. Counterdiscrimination by Negroes themselves is also a factor.

While data were not obtained on these matters in the 1958 survey, it seems safe to estimate that not less than 98 per cent of Detroit Negroes are married to others of their race and find their *close relatives* limited to their own race. With respect to *close friends*, it seems that an estimate of 90 to 95 per cent being limited to others of the Negro race would not be far wide of the mark.

To some extent the estimates above exaggerate the degree to which Negro Protestants associate with other Negro Protestants, since a small minority of the Negro population consists of Catholics, non-believers, and adherents of non-Christian cults. However, since these groups constitute no more than about 10–12 per cent of the Negro population, their influence is not great. Furthermore, most of these Negro minorities seem to share in the subculture of the dominant Negro Protestant majority.

While the associational bond in the Negro Protestant group is not nearly so strong as the communal bond, it is nevertheless stronger than in any of the other socio-religious groups except the white Catholic. Nearly 40 per cent of Negro Protestants attend worship services every Sunday, and more than three quarters attend at least once a month. Negro Protestants were tied with white Catholics in having the smallest percentage of persons who have completely divorced themselves from the nuclear religious associations. Only 5 per cent never go to church.

For a summary of the evidence so far we may turn to TABLE 1, which shows that each of our four groups possesses a distinctive combination of communal and associational attributes. Of the four, the white Protestant group seems to be the least cohesive, but is obviously in no danger of dissolution.

TABLE 1

RELATIVE STRENGTH OF ASSOCIATIONAL AND COMMUNAL BONDS IN THE FOUR MAJOR SOCIO-RELIGIOUS GROUPS

| Socio-religious Group | Strength of bonds: | |
	Associational	Communal
Jews	Weak	Strong
White Catholics	Strong	Medium
White Protestants	Medium	Medium
Negro Protestants	Medium	Strong

Social change and associational vitality

Will Herberg has argued that religious groups are becoming a more important feature of American life owing to basic changes in the nature of American society itself. For years America was the land of the immigrant, and so long as immigrants continued to pour into this country, the ethnic group provided them with an essential anchorage, a meaningful subcommunity in an increasingly impersonal mass society. While the ethnic churches and synagogues enjoyed an honored position in these groups, religious loyalties were generally less powerful than ethnic loyalties.

But, Herberg says, when the children of the immigrants reached maturity, a large number dissociated themselves from the ethnic subcommunity. It stood for something foreign and alien, and this "second generation" wanted above everything else to be a hundred-per-cent American. In rejecting the ethnic subcommunity, the second generation was obliged to reject also the church with which the subcommunity was inextricably linked. Hence, as the second generation became more numerous, interest in religion tended to decline.

However, Herberg argues that in recent years the second generation has begun to die off and the rising third generation does not need to strive to be American and to shed foreign and alien ways. It *is* American in every respect. Hence it can afford the luxury of reviving cultural patterns and loyalties abandoned by the second generation. In particular, it can afford to return to the church of its fathers.

This development is not only possible, but probable since, with the disintegration of the old ethnic subcommunities, Americans have a growing need for some *new* group to serve as an anchorage in modern society. Increasingly this anchorage is supplied by the religious groups. It is they which now provide the essential reference point from which the individual can relate himself to a mass society which, otherwise, threatens to reduce him to a statistical digit.

THE EVIDENCE RELEVANT TO HERBERG'S THESIS

In the 1958 Detroit Area Study we endeavored to test certain aspects of Herberg's theory, hoping not merely to check its validity but more especially to discover what is actually happening to the strength of the associational bond in the several socio-religious groups. Basically our findings confirm Herberg's thesis that the Americanization process is linked with the recent strengthening of religious associations, but several important modifications are necessary to make it conform to existing facts.

Among both white Protestants and white Catholics, the

third generation (unless otherwise indicated, this includes fourth and subsequent generations as well) was more active in the churches than the second generation, as Herberg predicted. However, our evidence did not support his hypothesis that the second generation is less active in the churches than the first. Only in the Jewish group was this tendency evident. Among white Protestants there was no difference in frequency of church attendance between these two generations, while among Catholics the second generation showed a marked increase in attendance over the first. Instead of the pattern of decline and return which Herberg speaks of, *our data suggest a pattern of increasing religious activity linked with increasing Americanization.* It should be added that further tests revealed that these differences are not a function of the age differences between the generations.

A second qualification to be made in Herberg's theory concerns intrasocietal migration. Southern-born white Protestant migrants to Detroit are no more active in the churches than first- or second-generation immigrants from abroad, even though in many cases they are sixth-, seventh-, eighth-, or more, generation Americans.

The explanation for this seems to be that the transition from the semirural South to a modern metropolitan community is in many respects a change comparable to that experienced by a first-generation immigrant from abroad. In short, activity in city churches seems most frequent among those who are not only the most Americanized but also the most urbanized. Since the trend is definitely towards a more Americanized and more urbanized population, it seems likely that these developments should strengthen the churches.

THE TRANSFORMATION OF THE CLASS SYSTEM

Another major consideration in any attempt to assess trends in associational involvement is the progressive transformation of the occupational and class structures of American society. For some years the proportion of the male, urban labor force in white-collar, or non-manual, positions has been slowly increasing with increasing mechanization and automation. Furthermore, not only has the middle class been increasing in size relative to the working class, but its social standards are permeating the working class more and more with each passing year, thanks to the growing influence of the mass media. As a result, an ever increasing number of people who are objectively manual workers think and act like members of the middle class. This is especially true of the upper stratum of the working class: skilled and supervisory workers. Therefore, those religious associations which are more successful in appealing to the middle classes should find the proportion of the total population actively involved in their organizations increasing in coming years. Conversely, those which have more appeal for the working classes may well experience some decline.

In all but the Jewish group the evidence indicates rather clearly that the middle classes are more highly involved in religious associations than the working classes. Among white Catholics, 74 per cent of the working class claimed to attend Mass every week, but among the middle class the figure was 82 per cent. For white Protestants, the corresponding figures were 23 and 32 per cent respectively, and for Negro Protestants 28 and 38 per cent.

In the case of the Jewish group the percentage of persons attending synagogue every week was greater in the working class than in the middle class, but owing to the limited number of cases in the 1958 sample the difference could have been due to sampling error. In an effort to determine whether the Jewish group actually differed from the other groups in this respect, data from the 1952, 1953, and 1957 samples were also examined and the results combined with those from the 1958 sample. Of the 68 middle-class Jewish respondents in these four samples, none reported attending services at synagogue or temple every Sabbath, though 19 per cent of the 26 working-class respondents did so. These figures suggest that the Jewish group may differ from other groups in this respect.

Reported changes in attendance during the last ten or fifteen years are also of special interest. Among *middle-class* whites of all groups who were *neither* first-generation immigrants *nor* southern-born, a *net gain* of 8 per cent in church attenders was indicated. Among comparable working-class whites a *net loss* of 6 per cent was reported. The greatest gains were found among middle-class whites of the fourth or later generations (excluding again the southern-born). In this category there was a *net gain of 26 per cent* in church attenders.

Such evidence suggests that the declining size of the working class and its increasing permeation by middle-class values will result in a rise in the percentage of persons active in the churches. This important trend therefore is likely to reinforce the influence of the Americanization and urbanization trend noted previously.

RISING LEVEL OF EDUCATION

A fourth social trend which promises increased associational involvement for at least the white Protestant and Catholic churches is the rising level of educational attainment. Among the white Protestants in our sample who had attended college, 41 per cent reported regular weekly attendance at worship services. Only 25 per cent of those with a high school education or less reported regular attendance. For Catholics the comparable figures were 86 and 74 per cent respectively. Among Negro Protestants and Jews the opposite pattern was indicated, but the number of college-trained persons in these groups was so small that extreme caution must be exercised in generalizing from the sample.

WORKING WIVES AND MOTHERS

Finally, one of the important trends in contemporary American society is the increasing tendency of married women to work outside the home. This is one development which could have serious consequences for the Protestant churches, both white and Negro. In both groups working wives were much less often active in the churches.

Since in the majority of American families the wife and mother plays the key role in stimulating religious interest and activity, this trend is one which cannot be ignored.

RELEVANCE OF TRENDS FOR THE CHURCHES

Putting together the various bits and pieces of evidence, we find that none indicate a decline in associational involvement among white Catholics, and several point to the opposite conclusion. The increasing Americanization of the population, the growth of the middle class, the permeation of the working class by middle-class values, and the rising level of education are all likely to cause an increase in the proportion of Catholics regularly attending Mass.

Prospects for the white Protestant churches are less clear-cut than for the Catholic churches. They should gain from the Americanization of the population, but not so much as the Catholics. The urbanization of the recent southern migrants and their children should benefit Protestantism far more than Catholicism, but these benefits may well be offset by continuing migration from the South. Protestantism should gain more than Catholicism from the rising level of education since college-trained white Protestants are more than half again as likely as those with less education to be regular churchgoers, whereas among Catholics the differential is approximately eight to seven. One important development however, is likely to work against any major increase in associational involvement—this is the trend toward increasing employment of women outside the home. The fact that, among white Protestants, working wives are so much less active could be a serious matter. Considering the combined influence of *all* these factors, it seems likely that there will be some increase in the proportion of white Protestants in Detroit attending church regularly during the next generation, but this increase should be somewhat less than the Catholic increase.

Our data indicate less optimistic predictions for Negro Protestants and Jews. Negro Protestant churches stand to gain nothing from the Americanization of the population, though the urbanization of the population could benefit them in the *long run*. In the short run, the continued migration of southern Negroes to northern cities seems likely to depress the rate of associational involvement. The growth of the Negro middle class might well benefit the Negro Protestant churches, but unfortunately available evidence strongly indicates that the Negro group may be the last to benefit from the transformation of the American economy. If the pattern of working wives becomes more common, this will hurt the Negro churches, and our data also suggest that the rising level of education may have the same effect. In short, the evidence indicates that in the next generation the percentage of Negro Protestants attending church regularly may well decline.

Finally, we come to the Jewish group. Almost all available evidence indicates a substantial decline in synagogue and temple attendance except on High Holy Days. However, in view of the strong communal ties uniting the members of this group (and probably also the secular associational ties) the group seems in little danger of assimilation or disintegration.

Social change and the subcommunities

As the present condition of the Jewish group indicates, it is not safe to infer the strength of communal ties from the strength of associational ties. Neither is it safe to infer trends in one from trends in the other. These two types of group involvement are sufficiently independent of one another for each to require separate analysis.

Since endogamy is the backbone of socio-religious communalism, changes in relevant attitudes or behavior are especially important in assessing trends in communalism. One of the questions we asked everyone was whether they thought it wiser for members of their group to marry within the group. The overwhelming majority of white respondents said that it *was* wiser. This was true of 92 per cent of the Jews, 81 per cent of the Catholics, and 75 per cent of the Protestants.

When the views of Detroiters were analyzed by immigrant generation, age, and class, those segments of the population which are growing in relative size were *more* committed to the principle of endogamy than those which are declining. For example, 80 per cent of the third-generation Americans thought it wiser for people to marry someone of their own faith, compared with 73 per cent of the first and second generation. Similarly, 83 per cent of the middle class, but only 66 per cent of the working class, shared this belief.

The communalistic tendency to limit *friendships* to one's own group was neither increasing nor declining in Detroit. The evidence indicated only that restrictive tendencies of this type are fairly stable and present patterns are likely to continue for the foreseeable future.

Summary

By way of summarizing all of the foregoing data, it appears that the major social trends of our time tend to strengthen both the associational and communal aspects of the two major socio-religious groups: the Catholic and white Protestant. As a minor qualification to this statement we should note that this strengthening apparently does not extend into the area of friendship, but is limited to marriage and kinship. In the case of the two smaller groups, the Negro Protestants and Jews, the nuclear associations seem to be weakened by current trends, but the data do not tell us how the subcommunities are being affected.

However, more important than any of these more specific conclusions is the general conclusion suggested by the evidence as a whole: contrary to the views and predictions of nineteenth-century positivists, *traditional religious groups continue to be viable and vigorous organizations.* What is more, they promise continued viability and vigor in the foreseeable future.

II. INTERGROUP IMAGES

Popular optimism often fails to reckon with the strength of the passions which communal loyalties and antagonisms can arouse. Here, as elsewhere, the potentiality for inter-group strife and violence exists.

Our aim in this section is to explore relationships among the groups at the level of the ordinary member. To accomplish this, we tried to discover what kind of *image* each of the groups has formed of the others. How do white Catholics look to white Protestants, and vice versa? What general characteristics do Negro Protestants attribute to Jews? Such images contain many facets, three of the more important being group tolerance, group honesty, and group power. For example, Protestants were asked:

1. Compared with Protestants, do you think Catholics as a whole are more tolerant, as tolerant, or less tolerant of the religious beliefs of other people?

2. Compared with Protestants, do you think Catholics as a whole are more fair, as fair, or less fair in their business dealings?

They were then asked a more general question about the power of Catholics:

3. Do you feel that Catholics have been trying to get too much power in this country, or not?

The same three questions were then repeated with comparisons made between Protestants and Jews.

When interviewing Catholic or Jewish respondents we used the same wording in the first two questions, simply reversing the names of the groups. On the question of power, a change in wording was introduced because historically Protestants have been the holders of power in American society. For Catholics and Jews the last question was worded:

Do you feel that Protestants have too much power in this country today, or not?

Unfortunately, in the planning stage of this study the need for differentiating between Negro and white Protestants was not so evident as it later became. Hence, parallel questions concerning white images of the Negro Protestant group were not obtained.

An unusually large number of Detroiters were unwilling to commit themselves on the questions about the tolerance, fairness, and power of other groups. Combining the responses to all of these questions, it was found that nearly one quarter were noncommittal. This was far above the average for other questions in the interview (typically 1 to 5 per cent).

There are two alternative explanations for this. The large number of noncommittal responses may reflect a judicious suspension of judgment by many Detroiters who realized they could not form valid judgments on such matters merely on the basis of personal experience (on the other hand, many people with strongly critical views of other groups may simply have been reluctant to sound "prejudiced" in front of a stranger).

Undoubtedly there were some instances of each of these two possibilities, but since Detroiters were generally willing to express opinions on a great variety of other subjects, the second hypothesis is probably the explanation in the majority of cases. This conclusion is also supported by the judgments of the interviewers.

White Protestants

Of all the groups, the white Protestants enjoyed the most favorable image in the eyes of others (see TABLE 2)[3] That is to say, Catholics have a more favorable image of Protestants than of Jews, and Jews have a more favorable image of Protestants than of Catholics. On each of the three criteria (religious tolerance, business fairness, and power), at least 60 per cent of both Catholics and Jews expressed approval of the white Protestants.

Although they were the least criticized, white Protestants were the most critical of other groups. As TABLE 5 indicates, they were especially critical of Catholics on the grounds of religious intolerance. They were least critical in the case of Catholic business practices.

To understand why Protestants were so often critical of

[3] We are assuming here that when Catholics and Jews make generalizations about "Protestants" they are usually thinking in terms of *white* Protestants. As noted previously, it would have been desirable to have made a racial distinction in these questions, but this need was not anticipated in advance.

other groups, but so seldom criticized themselves, it is necessary to remember that historically the United States has been a Protestant nation, in the sense that its culture and institutions were molded mainly by Protestants, and therefore inevitably expressed their viewpoints and values. As other groups have come into this country they have been at least partially assimilated to the Protestant-dominated secular culture. This means that they tend to judge Protestants by standards which are at least partially Protestantized, and therefore judge them more favorably than they judge other groups.

Also, Protestants have been the traditional holders of power. The continuance of this tradition is not likely to alarm other groups, providing only that their exercise of power allows aggressive and ambitious members of the newer groups to rise. In a society with democratic political institutions, and economic institutions which are becoming increasingly bureaucratized, such opportunities seem considerable. Hence, members of the newer groups are not overly critical or fearful of Protestant power.

From the Protestant standpoint, however, the situation looks quite different. Increasingly positions of power are being occupied by people whose commitment to traditional American standards, particularly those with a distinctively Protestant flavor, is not certain. Their rise may well lead to a transformation of the traditional institutional system; hence they are to be feared.

It also seems significant that white Protestants single out *different* characteristics of Catholics and Jews for criticism. They are twice as likely to criticize Jews for unfairness in business practices as for religious intolerance. This parallels the fact that the chief threat to Protestant power from the Jewish group is in the *economic* area. In the case of the Catholics, the situation is exactly reversed. They are criticized often for religious intolerance, but seldom for unfair business practices. Again, it seems more than coincidence that Catholic successes have been greater in the political than in the economic arena; hence

TABLE 2

PERCENTAGE EXPRESSING FAVORABLE IMAGE OF VARIOUS SOCIO-RELIGIOUS GROUPS WITH RESPECT TO TOLERANCE, BUSINESS FAIRNESS, AND POWER, BY SOCIO-RELIGIOUS GROUP

PERCENTAGE EXPRESSING FAVORABLE IMAGE* REGARDING:

Group Passing Judgment	Religious Tolerance			Business Fairness			Power			Mean
	of Prots.	of Caths.	of Jews	of Prots.	of Caths.	of Jews	of Prots.	of Caths.	of Jews	
White Protestants	—	30	49	—	71	47	—	49	56	50
Negro Protestants	—	44	49	—	64	39	—	63	44	51
White Catholics	60	—	54	78	—	45	68	—	58	61
Jews	65	31	—	62	68	—	73	65	—	61
Mean	63	35	51	70	68	44	71	59	53	56

* Responses were defined as favorable if the out-group was rated as equal with, or better than, the in-group in tolerance and fairness, and if the out-group was said not to be trying to get (or not having) too much power.

any tendencies toward religious intolerance are more of a threat when found in this group.

That white Protestant criticisms and fears are not wholly without foundation is indicated by certain other findings of this study. For example, nearly half of the white Catholic respondents in the 1958 sample said that they did not feel that the ministers of other churches should be allowed to teach publicly (as on the radio) things that are contrary to Catholic teaching. Another 10 per cent expressed uncertainty on this matter. Such widespread rejection of the American tradition of freedom of speech in such a large subgroup is bound to become known to white Protestants and cause fear and distrust. In this connection it is significant that nearly as many *Catholics* said that Catholics are *less* tolerant in religious matters than non-Catholics as said the reverse.

White Catholics

Catholics were much less critical and fearful of white Protestants than the latter were of them. However, it is interesting to note that Catholic criticisms of Protestants roughly paralleled Protestant criticisms of Catholics. Both groups were most critical of the other in the area of religious tolerance, and least critical in the area of business practices (see TABLE 2).

Catholics were consistently more critical of the Jews than of the white Protestants. This difference was especially marked in the area of business practices.

The most favorable image of the Catholic group was held by the Negro Protestant group. On all three items Negro Protestants were less critical of Catholics than either white Protestants or Jews. In fact, the only item on which any sizable number of Negro Protestants criticized the Catholic group was religious tolerance. The favorable image which Negro Protestants have formed of the Catholics is undoubtedly related to the strong stand the Catholic hierarchy has taken for racial integration. The fact that Catholic schools and churches have often been among the first to be integrated has not escaped the attention of the masses of Negro Protestants.

The Jewish group was much more critical of Catholics than the Negro Protestants were. In fact, they were nearly as critical as the white Protestants. Like both Protestant groups, the Jews most often criticized Catholics on the grounds of intolerance.

Jews

Of the three major white groups, the Jewish group was the most often criticized, and at the same time, the least critical of others. We have already noted the images which Jewish respondents had of other white groups, and the images which these other groups had of them. The Jews were somewhat less critical of the Protestants than were the Catholics, and they were also somewhat less critical of the Catholics than were the Protestants. This relatively favorable image was reciprocated by the white Protestants but not by the Catholics, who were much more critical of the Jews than of the Protestants.

The Negro Protestants resembled the Catholics far more than the white Protestants so far as their image of the Jewish group was concerned. This image was a highly critical one: in the frequency with which criticism was expressed it was second only to the white Protestant image of the Catholic group. Like other groups, Negro Protestants were most critical of Jewish business practices.

Throughout the critical comments of Gentiles, both white and Negro, certain themes constantly recurred. First, "the Jews are not trying to get power; they already have it." Second, "their power is economic and financial, not political." Third, "the Jews are less fair in their business dealings than non-Jews."

In the case of the Jewish group, it seems significant that to such a large degree its contacts with Gentiles occur in the context of the merchant-customer relationship. A study based on the 1952, 1955, and 1956 Detroit Area Studies combined revealed that nearly half of the Jewish family heads were self-employed compared with only 9 per cent of the rest of the population. This same study indicated that Jews were even more heavily concentrated in the ranks of retail merchants a generation earlier.

The Catholic and Protestant groups are far less vulnerable in this respect since the businessmen among their members are much more likely to be employees of some large, bureaucratized enterprise. The economic ethics of such concerns and their employees may be no better than those of small merchants, but ownership and control of most modern corporations is so diffuse or so hidden as to defy popular identification with any particular group.

The subcommunities, the churches, and intergroup images

Though the churches have often been accused of fostering intergroup tension and hostility, our evidence indicates that actually the subcommunities are the primary source of this in Detroit at present. As may be seen in TABLE 3, those who were most involved in the subcommunities were a good bit less likely to express favorable

TABLE 3

PERCENTAGE OF DETROITERS EXPRESSING FAVORABLE VIEWS OF SOCIO-RELIGIOUS GROUPS OTHER THAN THEIR OWN, BY SOCIO-RELIGIOUS GROUP, DEGREE OF COMMUNAL INVOLVEMENT, AND DEGREE OF ASSOCIATIONAL INVOLVEMENT

| | PERCENTAGE OF FAVORABLE VIEWS BY: | |
Type of Involvement: *Degree of Involvement*	*Catholics*	*White Prots.*
Involvement in Subcommunity		
Highly Involved	49	45
Other	62	54
Involvement in Church		
Highly Involved	53	53
Other	60	50

views of other groups than those who were not so involved.

By contrast, involvement in the churches had much less effect on images of other groups. In fact, in the case of Protestants, both Negro and white, those who were more active in the churches were a bit *more* likely to express favorable views of other groups than those who were less involved.

These findings underline the need for differentiating between the communal and associational aspects of socio-religious groups. They point up the fact that while socio-religious subcommunities are derivative from, and dependent on, religious associations (at least in modern societies), they are not mere appendages whose characteristics are dictated by the associations. On the contrary, the influence of the subcommunity on its members may be quite different from that of the religious association with which it is linked.

INTERFAITH MARRIAGES

Clark E. Vincent

Extent of Interfaith Marriages: It is very difficult at the present time to ascertain the extent of interfaith marriages in this country. Iowa is the only state which requires an indication of religious affiliation or preference on the marriage certificate, and Iowa has done so only since 1953. Thus we must rely on regional and denominational studies: some of which are reviewed briefly here.

The extent of interfaith marriages among Roman Catholics has been reported by Father John L. Thomas, a Jesuit and family sociologist at St. Louis University, who has compiled data from the official Catholic Directory, which lists interfaith marriages on an annual basis. Thomas has reported that during the decade 1940–50, approximately 30 per cent of all *valid* Catholic marriages (those sanctioned by the Church) involved a non-Catholic.[1] The Catholic Bishops' Committee on Mixed Marriages has estimated that between 15 and 25 per cent of all marriages involving Catholics are invalid—those usually involving a non-Catholic and not sanctioned by the Church.[2] Thus it would appear that at least one third of all Catholics who have married during the last two decades have contracted interfaith marriages.

A nationwide study initiated by the United Lutheran Church in America and based on a 12 per cent response

[1] John L. Thomas, "The Factor of Religion in Selection of Marriage Mates," *American Sociological Review,* XVI, August 1951, 487–491.

[2] Bishops' Committee on Mixed Marriages, *A Factual Study of Mixed Marriages* (Washington, D.C.: National Catholic Welfare Conference, 1943).

from 3319 pastors, indicated that 58 per cent of the Lutherans marrying between 1946 and 1950 had married a non-Lutheran.[3] Masters' theses on interfaith marriages among Mormons in Los Angeles, Oakland, and Berkeley, California, have shown the following percentages of Mormons marrying non-Mormons—20, 47, and 30.

The above are illustrative of the types of studies and findings that provide substance for the current concern over the extent of interfaith marriages. The data from such studies also suggest the degree to which the increase in church membership in this country may be a function of the multiple church membership of many individuals. For it has been estimated that one out of every three or four interfaith marriages results in one spouse changing to the other spouse's church. How many of these converted spouses are reported on the membership rolls of two or more churches?

The Trend in Interfaith Marriages: Only limited and tentative data are available on trends in interfaith marriages, but most of those that are available suggest an increase in such marriages. Father Thomas reports that there has been a gradual percentage increase in interfaith marriages among Catholics since 1910, and he predicts a gradual and steady increase in such marriages in the future. The Lutheran study referred to earlier indicates a similar trend—46 per cent of the Lutherans marrying between 1936 and 1940, but 58 per cent of the Lutherans marrying between 1946 and 1950, married non-Lutherans. The Mormon studies, completed in different cities, showed 20 per cent interfaith marriages in Los Angeles in 1937 and 47 per cent interfaith marriages in Oakland in 1955.

Patterns in Interfaith Marriages: Who married outside the church? Data in this area are also quite limited, and we shall make only brief reference to two types of findings—those on sex and socioeconomic differences. The studies referred to above on Catholics, Lutherans, and Mormons show that about three females marry outside

---

[3] James H. S. Bossard, and Harold C. Letts, "Mixed Marriages Involving Lutherans," *Marriage and Family Living*, XVIII, November 1956, 308–311.

the church for every two males who do so. Other studies have shown this pattern is reversed among Jews—about five males marry outside their faith for every two females who do so.[4] Such findings need to be interpreted quite cautiously, however, and need to be examined with reference to the male-female ratio within each of these religious groups.

With reference to socioeconomic differences, the data on Catholic as well as on Lutheran interfaith marriages have been interpreted to show that females who marry outside their church tend to marry above rather than below themselves socioeconomically. This tendency can be discussed with reference to several points: (a) it may be no greater than the tendency of females in the general population to marry males somewhat older, taller, better educated, etc., than themselves; (b) it may reflect what has been referred to as "church-hopping" or "church-shopping" as a means of social mobility; and (c) it may have relevance to the tentative findings from studies of interclass marriages, which suggest there is less marital strife when the wife marries above than when she marries below her own socioeconomic position. (These findings on interclass marriages have also been further interpreted as being consistent with the notion that wives do most of the adjusting in marriage and the notion that wives would sooner adjust "up" than "down." Thus marrying above themselves produces less marital friction than marrying below themselves.)

Reasons for or "Causes" of Interfaith Marriages: The research studies in this area can be grouped arbitrarily and reviewed briefly with reference to five "factors." The first factor is the disproportionate ratio of religious groups in a given community. Kennedy found three pots boiling merrily side by side, rather than one melting pot, in her studies of the New Haven community—Catholics married Catholics, Jews married Jews, and Protes-

[4] Judson T. and Mary G. Landis, *Building a Successful Marriage,* 3rd ed. (Englewood Cliffs, N.J.: Prentice Hall, 1958), Chapter 12, "Mixed Marriages."

tants married Protestants.[5] Such a finding, however, appears to be peculiar to New Haven and other communities where various religious groups are fairly well balanced, numerically. For Thomas found that in dioceses where Catholics represented about two thirds of the total community population, less than one fifth of the Catholics contracted interfaith marriages; but in dioceses where Catholics represented less than 5 per cent of the total community population, one half to three fourths of the Catholics married non-Catholics. The significance of this factor is also supported by data on interfaith marriage among Mormons. In 1937 Done reported that in Salt Lake City, where Mormons then represented almost three fourths of the city's population, less than 7 per cent married non-Mormons.[6] In 1957 Follett reported that in Oakland and Berkeley, where Mormons represented less than 5 per cent of the total community population, 47 and 30 per cent had married non-Mormons.[7]

A second factor is the disproportionate male-female ratios in the several social strata *within* any one church. This involves the unavailability within one's own church of those mates who have been sanctioned by mate-selection mores as being desirable. In general, our society tends to sanction and encourage marriages of women to men slightly superior to them in age, education, and social status. When such men are in short supply within the women's particular church, there is an increased tendency to select marital partners outside the church. The Lutheran study cited earlier, for example, noted that the lower the social status of the Lutheran parish in a given community, the higher the percentage of the parish's members who

[5] Ruby Jo. Reeves Kennedy, "Single or Triple Melting Pot? Intermarriage Trends in New Haven, 1870–1940," *American Journal of Sociology*, XLIX, January 1944, 331–339; and *American Journal of Sociology*, LVIII, July 1952, 56–66.

[6] G. Byron Done, "A Study of Mormon-Gentile Intermarriages in Los Angeles," Unpublished Master's thesis, University of Southern California, 1937.

[7] Elizabeth Nicholson Follett, "A Study of Interfaith Marriages Among Mormons in Berkeley, California," Unpublished Master's thesis, University of California, Berkeley, 1958.

marry non-Lutherans. A sizable proportion of those who marry outside their church in such cases tend to be women who marry above their own socioeconomic status. Such findings have been interpreted as evidence that interfaith marriages represent a means of upward social mobility for women; but it needs to be kept in mind that the mate-selection mores in our society tend to prescribe marriages involving some upward mobility for women—whether those marriages represent interfaith, interclass, or rural-urban mixtures.

A third factor is our mass participation in a so-called middle-class culture; wherein our individual as well as group differences in values and religious beliefs tend to be minimized if not obscured by a superficial amalgamation. This factor, which may well be one of the most important in understanding the current increase in interfaith marriages, is not easily quantified. Thus I can only make reference to some of the areas and ways in which this factor appears to be operative. Today's youth on high school and college campuses tend to use this so-called middle class as their reference group and behavior guide. The ideology and behavior patterns of this somewhat mythical reference group are disseminated to today's youth through mass media of entertainment and communication, as well as through textbooks which report findings on the mate-selection patterns of primarily middle-class subjects. The efforts to emulate and to be considered "middle class," combined with the considerable residential mobility and commuting distances of today's youth, tend to preclude dating couples' realistic appreciation of their differences in family and religious backgrounds. As Margaret Mead has noted, young dating couples today rarely know even a dog in common from childhood days.

This current tendency to act as if we were all very similar, and to subsequently blur individualistic and familial backgrounds, also points up the considerable evaluational task that is assigned to modern dating. In the small community and rural orientation of this country a few generations ago, the family performed many of the functions which today's dating couple perform increasingly by themselves. Yesterday, Susie's parents knew Joe's parents (on what side of the tracks they lived, if and where they attended church, and the shape and magnitude of family skeletons), and over a period of years could attempt to influence Susie's answer to Joe by imparting first-hand knowledge of his background. Today, Susie's parents have to rely on Joe for any information about his family background, and to hope that Susie will let them meet Joe before she gives him her answer. Thus, today's dating couple tries to accomplish during a few months or a year the evaluational tasks on which the extended family of yesterday worked for a period of years and to which the church contributed by publishing "banns."

Summarily with reference to this third factor, it is surprising that there are no more interfaith marriages than there are when we consider the "middle-class ethic" with its obscuring of origin and background as an implied test for membership; the current earlier age at marriage; the multiple tasks assigned to dating; and the tendency to replace personal religious convictions with "scientific objectivity." An even greater miracle is that today's youth are able within such contexts to choose their marital partners so well.

A fourth factor is that couples may contract interfaith marriages on the basis of nationality and cultural similarities. For example, we would expect more interfaith marriages between Lutherans and Catholics in a community composed primarily of people of German extraction, than we would in a community composed of German Lutherans and Italian Catholics. This factor needs to be kept in mind not only when considering what brings together couples from different religious backgrounds, but also when considering the degree of marital strife that may be associated with interfaith marriages. Many times when we think we are talking about or studying "pitfalls" of interfaith marriages, we may really be addressing the by-products of nationality and cultural differences.

The fifth factor represents a composite of adolescent rebellion and disaffiliation from a minority culture. Examination of this factor in the search for "causes" of interfaith marriages, has been confined primarily to case-history materials. The interpretations and reconstruction of the materials in these case histories frequently reflect the notion of "heads, I win; tails, you lose." When the focus is on the member of a majority culture who marries a member of a minority culture, the interpretation tends to point out how the former is using such a marriage to "act out" rebellion and resentment against parental or other superego restraints. When the focus is on the member of a minority culture who marries a member of a majority culture, the interpretation tends to point out how the former is using such a marriage to improve his or her social status. Valid as such interpretations may be in some instances, they reflect the tendency to view intermarriages in areas of prejudice as being caused by "bad" or at least negative factors. They also reflect our reluctance to admit that the contractants to interfaith and interracial marriages can be motivated positively by mutual love and respect.

Consequences of Interfaith Marriage: This is the area in which we find the greatest amount of interest, writing, and research, but probably the least complete information. There are two major rationales for the concern in this area. First is the membership leakage which results from interfaith marriages. Jewish writers have noted that such marriages have depleted Jewish ranks more than persecutions. The Catholic Bishops' Committee on Mixed Marriages has reported that 30 per cent of the Catholics involved in interfaith marriages are lost to the Catholic Church. Studies of interfaith marriages involving Protestants show that between one third and one half of the contractants to such marriages withdraw from their original church.

The second major rationale for the interest in the consequences of interfaith marriages is the relations of such marriages to divorce. Three studies conducted independently in different states have shown similar findings which are summarized below: one study of 13,528 cases was conducted in Maryland; another study of 4108 cases was conducted in Michigan; and the third study of 6548 cases was conducted in Washington.

Religious categories	Per cent ending in divorce or separation
Both Catholic	5 per cent
Both Jewish	5 per cent
Both Protestant	8 per cent
Mixed, Catholic-Protestant	15 per cent
Both none	18 per cent

It must be pointed out that the "both Protestant" marriages result in more divorces and separations than the "both Catholic" or "both Jewish" marriages, because the category of "both Protestants" probably includes many interdenominational marriages.

The limitations of using such figures as the basis of broad generalizations concerning the dangers of Catholic-Protestant intermarriages has been illustrated by Judson Landis, who was the only one of the above three researchers to explore these data further.[8] He found that 7 per cent of the total 90 mixed marriages involving a Catholic wife, and a Protestant husband ended in divorce or separation: but 21 per cent of the total 102 mixed marriages involving a Catholic husband and a Protestant wife ended in divorce or separation.

Two interpretations have been given for this difference. (a) Since approximately three fourths of all divorce proceedings are initiated by wives, and since the Catholic Church takes a more stringent position on divorce than do most Protestant churches, the mixed marriages involving a Catholic wife will result in fewer divorces than those involving a Protestant wife. (b) Since the Ante-Nuptial Agreement requires that the children of the marriage be reared in the Catholic faith, and since mothers tend to be more active than fathers in child-rearing, the Protestant mother would find the Ante-Nuptial Agreement less palatable than would the Protestant father.

[8] Judson T. and Mary G. Landis, *Building a Successful Marriage*, 3rd ed. (Englewood Cliffs, N.J.: Prentice Hall, 1958), Chapter 12, "Mixed Marriages."

Summary Limitations of data on Interfaith Marriage:
It is perhaps necessary to emphasize that the statistical
data on interfaith marriages and divorce show associations, not "causes." Even when those associations are
higher than might occur by chance, they still do not
indicate "cause," any more than a very high statistical
association between storks and a high birth rate in some
rural regions, and the association between no storks and
the lowest birth rate in the nation in such a city as San
Francisco, can be used to prove that babies are brought
by storks. As noted earlier, we do not know the extent
of divorce among intradenominational marriages. Nor do
we know whether the divorces occurring among interfaith marriages are related primarily to religious differences or to socioeconomic, nationality, and cultural differences. Moreover, we do not have a very clear picture of
the extent of divorce in the total population with which
to compare the extent of divorce in interfaith marriages.
In some studies each divorce involving two partners is
counted as one case. In other studies each partner is
counted as a separate case. Recidivists may be counted
many times.

This statistical murkiness is not just of academic interest; it is related to the question which is sometimes
raised as to whether the concern of religious bodies about
interfaith marriages is primarily a concern for the individuals involved or whether the concern for the individual
is a by-product of the concern for the numerical growth
of the church. Even a cursory glance at the denominational literature on the subject of interfaith marriages
evinces a primary concern about the membership leakage
which is believed to result from such marriages. This
concern is usually stated in terms of divorce, marital
strife, lack of religious instruction for the children, etc.,
but figures and comments concerning the numerical loss
to the church are seldom lacking.

Suppose that more complete and thorough research
should show that the incidence of divorce and the
amount of marital strife are as great in intradenominational as in interdenominational marriages, would church

members then be warned against marrying those of their own faith? Also, if roughly one third of those who marry outside the church are "lost to the *church*" how many of the other two thirds who remain in the church convert their non-member spouse? If research should show that interfaith marriages actually augment membership goals, would such marriages continue to be discouraged and warned against?

Indeed there may be a circular phenomenon involved here, wherein a high rate of divorce for interfaith marriages may partly result from the opposition to such marriages by religious bodies which offer as one of the reasons for their opposition a high rate of divorce. Many of the difficulties experienced in interfaith marriages may be symptoms or manifestations of the failure of organized religion to "lose itself" as an institution.

In Western society our religious heritage is permeated with polarization (the concept of mutual exclusion) whether in the earlier more explicit terms of people who were either among the "elect" or the "damned"; or in the current more implicit terms of the sacerdotal forms and modes of worship which are either "rite" or "wrong." As long as organized religion continues to indoctrinate its members with the notion that there is only one way and one church, couples in interfaith marriages will find that loyalty to the church will preclude granting the reality of the spouses' beliefs. Differences that could enlarge and enrich both their religious commitments, become stimuli for marital disharmony and threats to each other's beliefs.

RELIGION AND POLITICS
IN AMERICAN HISTORY*

Seymour Martin Lipset

When one is seeking to analyze what makes people behave differently, whether it be their work habits, parent-child relationships, size of family, achievement aspirations, or whatever, religion must be included among the list of explanatory variables. At the least, religious denominations must be regarded as subcultural units that serve as important reference groups for their members. These are the social groups whose approbation a member seeks, or from whom he takes his standards of judgment in many aspects of behavior. And political behavior clearly falls into the area of those heavily linked to religious background. There are at least three kinds of variation among religious groups that bear on their political differentiation:

1. *Different Social Characteristics*. Different church groupings have definable differences in the socioeconomic and ethnic composition as well as in the geography of their memberships.

2. *Different Historical Experiences*. The Episcopalian and Congregationalist churches were state-established churches in early America; the Baptist and Methodist churches were not. In the 1930s, world Jewry was under attack by Adolf Hitler. These secular experiences have had a relationship to political identification.

3. *Different Religious Values*. Different religious groups vary in religious ideology in such spheres as public morality and social welfare. Methodists and Baptists have been

concerned with the evils inherent in liquor and gambling; Catholics reject birth control and divorce as sinful.

The close interdependence of these three factors for any given religious group is obvious. It is the continuing task of religious history and sociology to probe the shifting relationship among these factors, but it is sufficiently clear that they have operated to make religious variation a matter of political significance in America.

THE BASIC DESIGN

The Formative Years

America's first experience with political differentiation among religious groups began with the founding of the nation. The Episcopalian and Congregationalist churches became identified with the conservative Federalists and Whigs, while the Baptist, Methodist, and Presbyterian churches were linked with the Jeffersonians and Jacksonians. Initially, this divergence was in some part the result of the different social characteristics of these religious groups, and in some part related to the fact that the former had been state-established churches.

The more traditionalistic Federalists were concerned with maintaining various values and behavior patterns that persisted from English times, and many of them favored the preservation of established religions. The Congregationalist Church was the established church for many years in the Federalist strongholds, New Hampshire until 1817, Connecticut until 1818, and Massachusetts until 1833.

The defeat of the Federalists, first in the South where the Jeffersonians were dominant, then later in New England, was related to the disestablishment of the churches. It should be noted that while there was, in this period, a decline of religious institutions generally, the elimination of established religion was not in itself a defeat of religion; the Protestant denominations that were *not* established predictably supported the disestablishment of the state church.

The resolution of the establishment issue in the early nineteenth century did not end the relationship between various denominations and party politics. Evidence drawn from an analysis of voting records would suggest that the link between the traditional high-status churches, Anglican and Congregationalist, and the more conservative party continued after the demise of the Federalists. Conversely those denominations that were associated with lower status groups, either in terms of ethnic origins, more recent immigrant status, or class composition, tended to be identified with the Democrats. Catholics, largely Irish, though not the major force they were later to become, were nevertheless a noticeable group in some of the larger cities such as Boston and New York, and then as later were largely Democratic.

The linkage between Catholics, plus others of more recent immigrant stock, and the Democratic party was cemented at this early period in American history by the fact that the Federalists openly and avowedly tried to make life difficult for them, while the Jeffersonians defended their interests and rights.

All the studies of voting behavior during this period agree that religious affiliation played a major role in differentiating the supporters of the two parties. The most detailed of them, that by Manning Dauer covering elections around 1800, reports that the Federalist party benefited considerably from Congregationalist support.[1] The Episcopalians who had been the established church in the southern States also gave heavy backing to the conservative party. "The other religions whose members originally supported the Federalists were the German Reformed, Dutch Reformed, and Lutheran denominations . . . the Quakers, strongest in Pennsylvania, were gener-

---

[1] Manning Dauer, *The Adams Federalists* (Baltimore: Johns Hopkins Press, 1953), p. 25. See also Anson Stokes, *Church and State in the United States* (New York: Harper, 1950), I, pp. 408–410.

ally Federalist, except when war threatened."[2] In areas
which backed the Jeffersonians "the chief denominations
were the Baptists . . . the Methodists and Presbyterians
. . . concentrated in the back country geographically; and
these same denominations plus the Irish Catholics in the
towns."[3] It is difficult to estimate the extent to which
such apparent differences in denominational political
allegiance were directly related to the interest or theological positions of the churches, or reflected variations
in socioeconomic position. The denominations that backed
the Democrats all had an "interest" in disestablishment;
they were largely composed of the less well-to-do; the
Baptists and the Methodists were new sects whose
ministers and adherents ranked low in the social hierarchy;
the Presbyterians were largely a low-status Scotch-Irish
immigrant group who had been rejected by the Puritans
of New England and "were natural recruits for a leveling
party."[4]

One would expect, however, that these groups would be
among the most moralistic, and dislike the secularistic
attitudes and policies of the many Democratic leaders
who were Deists and generally indifferent to the traditional religions. The binding link between the "out-group"
sects and the Deist party leaders would seem to have
been a common dislike against the power and influence
of the once established or traditional denominations.

Whig spokesmen, like the Federalists before them,
gave voice to the values of the dethroned Puritan establishment. They argued that the state was a proper instrument to eradicate moral evils such as gambling and
"grogselling," while the Jacksonian Democrats sought to
limit the role of the state to the prevention of evils that

[2] Ibid., pp. 28–29.
[3] Loc. Cit., on the Irish, see Carl Wittke, *The Irish in
America* (Baton Rouge: Louisiana State University Press,
1956), p. 106.
[4] See Lawrence H. Fuchs, "Some Political Aspects of Immigration," in Joseph Piszman, ed., *The American Political
Arena* (Boston: Little, Brown, 1962), p. 523 for a discussion
of the role of the Scotch-Irish as "the core ethnic group of the
Democratic Party."

resulted from individuals or groups being interfered with by others. The religious feeling and action that underlay the Federalist and Whig moralistic concerns may be seen in the activities of Lyman Beecher who as a key figure in the Congregationalist Church also was involved successively in Federalist, Whig, and later Republican politics. He, like many others of the New England theocrats, "sought to establish a clerically dominated social order by means of voluntary social and moral reform societies that would give the clergy an influential role in forming public opinion and molding public legislation. The many "benevolent societies of the [Jacksonian] Period, which sought to evangelize the unchurched, to save the heathen, to sober the drunkard, to rescue the wayward female, to purify the Sabbath, to end dueling, to inaugurate Sunday Schools, and to send freed slaves back to Africa . . . [were composed largely of] the ministers and leading laymen and women of the Congregational churches."[5]

The party struggle was clearly not between religion and irreligion, although apparently most freethinkers and their organizations supported the Democrats while the very devout established groups—particularly among the older ones—backed the Whigs.

It is important to recognize that there was considerable congruence between the Jacksonian concern for secular equalitarianism and the struggle against the domination of the theocracy in religion. As McLoughlin puts it: "Here was the essence of the quarrel between the Whigs and the Jacksonians: the fight against aristocracy and privilege in politics had a clear parallel in religion."[6]

The Great Re-Alignment

The early religious-political pattern in America, therefore, found the more evangelical Protestants, particularly

[5] William G. McLoughlin, "Introduction," Charles G. Finney, *Lectures on Revivals of Religion* (Cambridge: Belknap Press of Harvard University Press, 1950), p. XVII.

[6] Op. cit., p. XIX.

the Baptists, the Methodists, and the Presbyterians backing the Jeffersonians-become-Democrats, along with the emerging Catholic population. The more deeply established and less evangelical Protestants, notably the Congregationalists and the Episcopalians supported the Federalists and Whigs-become-Republican. But by the time the two-party system had been recast in its durable Republican-Democratic mold after the Civil War, the northern Methodists, Presbyterians, and Baptists were predominantly Republican. Since most American Protestants had by then become Baptists and Methodists, this realignment meant that native-born Protestants in general had become predominantly Republican.

There were, of course, a number of reasons for the shift of these several Protestant bodies. To begin with, both their socioeconomic level in society and their symbolic status rose rapidly. The high-status churches, Episcopal, Congregational, Quaker, and Unitarian, had not participated in the evangelical revivalism and expansion which the other Protestant groups underwent during the first half of the nineteenth century. The once-established churches remained disproportionately concentrated in the cities of the East, and declined in relative numerical importance. At the same time the influx of Roman Catholic immigrants, especially the Irish, swelled the working class. Thus, in terms of relative standing in the social scale, Methodists and Baptists were both pulled and pushed upward. Simultaneously, these groups underwent in varying degrees the familiar shift from sect to denomination, a shift which was consonant with the forces changing their social position from without. In fact, these groups attained something of the status of "established churches" themselves. By 1850, two thirds of the Protestants were Baptists and Methodists. Both groups had a sizable middle-class membership, and the Methodists possessed considerable urban strength.

With the improvement in numbers and influence of these ascendant Protestant groups went a corresponding increase in willingness to use state power to enforce "their morality." There was still a kind of parallel between the fight against the political establishment and the fight against the (now unofficial) religious establishment, but the Baptists and Methodists began to move to the "other side" of the fight as they became more "established" themselves. They joined older-established Protestant churches and the prevailing conservative political party in raising moral concerns as public issues. A purely religious dimension entered as a differentiating factor here. The Episcopalian Church (like the Lutheran and the Catholic churches) had come out of a tradition of having been a state and total-society church, and never did see its religious mission as prescribing behavior, in the way that the sects or denominations with sectarian origin typically do. Thus, in the early part of the nineteenth century, the surge of organizational movements to raise public morality—e.g., for temperance, peace, abolition of slavery, and maintenance of the Sabbath—were predominantly fostered by members of the old Federalist upper class and Congregational ministers, aided by the Presbyterians.

For example, the early nineteenth-century concern with the drinking habits and general state of morality among the population had strong class and political links. "The Federalists reasoned that if they could wean men from profanity, vice and inebriation, the former sinners would be amenable to changing their political allegiance."[7] Reports of the day indicate that temperance and Federalism were closely identified by friends and foes alike.

The early temperance movement was dominated by members of the old Calvinist denominations, but its social base began to change in the 1840s. The rising evangelical sects also turned against the sin of drink. It was "becoming a potent sign of middle class status, distinguishing the abstainer from the lower levels of the ne'er-do-wells, the unambitious and the irreligious."[8]

[7] Clifford S. Griffin, *Their Brothers' Keepers* (New Brunswick: Rutgers University Press, 1960), p. 37: John A. Krout, *The Origins of Prohibition* (New York: 1925), pp. 83–100.

[8] Joseph Gusfield, "Status Conflicts and the Changing Ideologies of the American Temperance Movement," in David

As a matter of fact, the Baptists and the Methodists called for more drastic measures than did the earlier temperance leaders. The former favored total abstinence and eventually the passage of prohibition legislation, whereas the latter had advocated education to secure moderate drinking.

Similarly, the leadership of the abolitionist organizations, begun in the 1830s was drawn from substantial upper middle class and distinguished Federalist families, predominantly Congregational, Presbyterian, and Quaker, even though they included many Methodists, and were supported of course by Transcendentalist-Unitarian intellectuals. However, a number of studies have associated the subsequent mass growth of the anti-slavery movement in the North with the emergent evangelical denominations. Abolition had particular strength in areas where there had been successful revivalist campaigns.

While the more evangelical denominations fostered abolitionist sentiment in the North, it is significant to note that membership in the very same churches was related to support for slavery in the South. Thus the three churches that split into northern and southern wings were the Presbyterians, Baptists, and Methodists. The Presbyterians suffered their first division in 1837–38. "Although the split of New School and Old School was ostensibly along theological lines, in fact the South remained with the Old School and the alliance of abolitionism and revivalism shaped the New School General Assembly."[9]

The Baptists and Methodists also separated long before the Civil War as a result of "contrasting attitudes on the part of the two sections of the church (North and South) on a moral question, slavery."[10] The positions of each of these evangelical denominations on opposite sides of the abolition question partly reflect the "settling in" of these

Pittman and Charles A. Snyder, eds., *Society, Culture and Drinking Practices* (New York: John Wiley, 1962), p. 107.

[9] Franklin H. Littell, *From State Church to Pluralism* (Garden City: Doubleday Anchor Books, 1962), p. 64.

[10] H. Richard Niebuhr, *The Social Sources of Denominationalism* (New York: Meridian Books, 1957), p. 194.

groups, North and South, and their consequent support of their respective political establishments. It is notable, however, that abolition was an issue that lent itself to deep "moral" feeling on both sides, and was therefore one in which those denominations were able to commit themselves more thoroughly and with more religious vehemence than the Episcopalian, the Catholic, or the Lutheran bodies.

The clue to understanding these reactions lies in the attitudes towards sin that had emerged among the deeply religious evangelical American Protestants:

> The most significant characteristic of the Protestant attitude was consciousness of the evil nature of sin. Protestant expounders made a simple and clear-cut distinction between right and wrong. Man was either saved or damned. Righteousness would be rewarded, sin punished. Sin must be fought. . . .

> Urged on by conscience, the dissatisfied soon found that the (basic community) sin was the sin of slavery. This cancer of society should be cut out, and stern duty called upon foes of sin to remove it . . . These intense foes of the South were going to do everything possible to destroy slavery. They found their duty all the more compelling as the sin was largely in the body politic of the South, and attack upon it must weaken those who held power.[11]

Just as evangelical Protestantism helped to make the conflict "irrepressible" by bolstering the moral fiber of abolitionism, it served the same role south of the Mason and Dixon line by defining the sectional conflict as one of God versus Satan as well.

Whatever other effects issued from this deep commitment of the major Protestant groups to the abolitionist issue, it certainly served both to facilitate and to dramatize their great realignment with the Republican party in the North and West.

The temperance and prohibition issues also played a

[11] Roy Franklin Nicholas, *The Disruption of American Democracy* (New York: Collier Books, 1962), pp. 35, 43.

major and interrelated role in recruiting evangelical Protestants to the anti-Democratic ranks. To a considerable extent, those active in abolition groups also strongly backed prohibitionist organizations, and vice versa. Antislavery candidates were often also advocates of prohibition. "In the 1850's, various combinations of antislaveryism, antiforeignism, and prohibitionism were electing hundreds of . . . men to office."[12]

But if these interrelated moral issues associated with the parties of the well-to-do and better educated resulted in defections from the Democrats of native-born adherents of the evangelical sects, the Democrats were able to recoup their losses from the heavy waves of immigration.

The Democrats, as opposed to the Whigs and the Republicans, were much more oriented to serving the needs of the poor and new immigrants; they tended to oppose restrictions on liquor, whereas as we have seen their opponents supported them; and perhaps most important of all as far as the immigrants and Catholics were concerned, the Whigs and Republicans were often explicitly allied with various nativist and anti-Catholic organizations, such as the Native Americans and the Know-Nothings.

When the anti-foreign, anti-Catholic Know-Nothings broke up over the slavery question, the vast majority of them seem to have joined the Republicans in the North. Election data indicate that they had "served as a bridge between the old Whig party and the Republican party."[13]

Before the 1860 presidential elections Republican midwestern leaders, including Lincoln, made valiant efforts to destroy the impression that the party was anti-Catholic or anti-foreign, since in addition to the principle of equality itself, many of them realized that the foreign-born vote, particularly the German, could lose them the

[12] Griffin, op. cit., p. 220.
[13] Lawrence F. Schmeckebier, History of the Know-Nothing Party in Maryland, "Studies in Historical and Political Science, Johns Hopkins University, 17 (1899), p. 40; Wilfred Binkley, American Political Parties, Their Natural History (New York: Knopf, 1947), p. 103.

election if it went decisively against them. A detailed analysis of voting returns in Wisconsin indicates that this Republican effort which was led by Carl Schurz was unsuccessful. The Wisconsin Domesday Book project, "a superior Gallup Poll," indicates that five sixths of the Germans backed Douglas against Lincoln, "because of the Know-Nothing nativism which the Republicans had absorbed."[14]

In the late nineteenth and early twentieth centuries, outside of the one-party South, the anti-Catholic and anti-immigrant politics that continued to exist tended to find a home inside of the Republican party. And on the issue of Catholic efforts to secure state funds for parochial schools, "often the local and state Democratic parties became allied with the Catholic point of view or at least were not hostile," while the Republicans took "the opposite stand."[15] "Running for governor of Ohio in 1875, Rutherford B. Hayes worked fiercely to smear the Democrats as subservient to Catholic designs. President Grant struck a similar campaign note at a veterans' reunion that fell by hinting darkly that unless the public schools were kept free from sectarian influence the nation might face a new civil war between the forces of patriotism and intelligence on the one side and superstition and ignorance on the other. . . . During the election of 1876 occasional Republican[s] charg[ed] that the 'Romanish Church' was using the Democratic party to overthrow the American school system. . . ."[16]

It should not be surprising that a recent study of immigrant groups concludes that the two major Catholic ethnic groups, the Irish and the German, remained loyal to

---

[14] See Joseph Schafer, "Who Elected Lincoln," *American Historical Review*, 47, October 1941, p. 51. Lincoln's advocacy of abstinence and prohibition legislation in Illinois could not have endeared him to the German voters.

[15] R. Freeman Butts, *The American Tradition in Religion and Education* (Boston: The Beacon Press, 1950), p. 142.

[16] John Higham, *Strangers in the Land* (New Brunswick: Rutgers University Press, 1955), pp. 28–29; Anson Stokes, *Church and State in the United States* (New York: Harper, 1950), II, p. 68.

the Democratic party for the half-century after the Civil War. The former, of course, played an increasingly important role within the party organization in the large cities, while like "their Irish co-religionists, German Catholics tended to regard the Republican party as a vehicle for intolerant Puritans bent on prohibition, Sunday closing, and immigration restriction."[17]

THE DESIGN AT WORK: THE TWENTIETH CENTURY

The basic religious-political pattern crystallized in the latter part of the nineteenth century was one of increasing Catholic identification with the Democratic party as the party least antipathetic to newcomers and increasing Protestant identification with the Republican party as the party most closely allied with the American middle-class *status quo* of the time.

Following the Civil War, the link between Protestant orthodoxy and Americanism as a political ideology became closer than ever. The victory of the North was taken by many in the northern church as clear evidence that they had been fighting God's crusade and "it was but another short step to the enshrinement of the political instrument which, in the hands of Providence, had guided the Union to victory over slavery and disunion."[18]

Sidney Mead concludes that there is general agreement among historians "that at the time Protestantism in America achieved its greatest dominance of the culture (the second half of the nineteenth century), it had also achieved an almost complete ideological and emotional identification with the burgeoning bourgeois society and its free enterprise system, so that in 1876 Protestantism

[17] Maldwyn Jones, *American Immigrants* (Chicago: University of Chicago Press, 1960), p. 166.
[18] Sidney E. Mead, "American Protestantism Since the Civil War: From Denominationalism to Americanism," in Abraham Eisenstad, ed., *American History, Book II: Since 1865* (New York: Thomas Y. Crowell, 1962), p. 174.

presented a massive, almost unbroken front in its defense of the social status quo. . . ."[19]

James Bryce probably represented the consensus of informed opinion on the subject in the post-Civil War period, when he reported as of the 1880s: "Roman Catholics are normally Democrats, because, except in Maryland, which is Democratic anyhow, they are mainly Irish. Congregationalists and Unitarians, being presumably sprung from New England, are apt to be Republicans. Presbyterians, Methodists, Baptists, Episcopalians . . . are mostly Republicans in the Northern States, Democrats in the South."[20] It is, however, difficult to be precise concerning the relationship between party support and religious and ethnic group memberships from the Civil War to the Smith campaign in 1928. Historians, political scientists, and sociologists have in the main failed to analyze the basic data. The existing research does indicate, however, that lines of division held fairly firmly during these decades.

It is true that entry into war under Wilson resulted in a major alienation of traditional Democratic Irish and Catholic support. In 1920, the Republicans won their greatest victory in history, securing 61.2 per cent of the national vote.

James M. Cox, the Democratic candidate in that year, has himself well described what happened to him and his party:

> Leaders of three racial groups, Germans, Irish and Italian, had gone over to the Republican side. The Germans were angry with Wilson because of the war. The Irish were inflamed because Wilson did not make the independence of Ireland part of the Versailles treaty. The Italians were enraged

---

[19] Ibid., pp. 186, 187.
[20] James Bryce, *The American Commonwealth*, Vol. II (Toronto: The Copp, Clark Company, 1891), p. 36. Bryce also mentions that the support of the Democrats by "the Roman Catholic Germans [is due] to the tacit alliance which has subsisted in many districts between the Catholic Church and the Democrats."

because Fiume had been taken away from Italy. The Italians were practically solid.[21]

In 1924, the Democrats remained weak among the groups which had defected in 1920. Many of them voted for Senator Robert LaFollette, on a third-party ticket. He had been a major leader in resisting entry into the war, had campaigned vigorously for the independence of Ireland, and perhaps most important of all, was the presidential candidate most avowedly opposed to the Ku Klux Klan, and most denounced by the Klan.

The rise of the Ku Klux Klan to prominence during the 1920s undoubtedly played an important role in preventing the Republicans from making permanent inroads among disaffected Democrats of Catholic and recent immigrant background. In much of the Northeast and Midwest, the Klan, like the American Protective Association before them, largely worked through the Republican party and had considerable influence in some of the state organizations. "In the East, where the Democratic Party was controlled largely by Irish Catholics, the Klan inevitably associated itself more closely with the Republicans."[22] In addition, the Republicans had fostered both Prohibition and quota restrictions on immigration that were biased in favor of entrants from the Nordic Protestant nations, while the northern Democratic members of Congress had shown opposition to these measures that were clearly unpalatable to most Catholics and others of recent immigrant stock.

The decline of the Democrats in presidential voting, particularly among Catholics and recent immigrant groups, did not mean that the party had lost its following among them. Some political analysts who have focused only on the presidential races have erred in suggesting that

21 James M. Cox, *Journey Through My Years* (New York: Simon and Schuster, 1946), pp. 272–273.

22 Samuel Lubell, *The Future of American Politics* (Garden City: Doubleday Anchor Books, 1956), p. 89; see also Emerson Hunsberger Loucks, *The Ku Klux Klan in Pennsylvania* (Harrisburg: the Telegraph Press, 1936), p. 99; John B. Martin, *Indiana* (New York: Knopf, 1947), pp. 193–194.

strong Catholic Democratic loyalties stem from 1928, the year Al Smith ran for President. They overlook the fact that the Democratic vote for state offices in many areas with large Catholic populations remained extremely high in the years during which the party declined heavily on the presidential level. Thus in Massachusetts in 1922, the Democratic percentage of the two-party vote for governor was 17.6 higher than in the 1920 presidential race. And the party gained much more in cities that had a large majority of foreign-born population than it did in communities that were predominantly native-born. Similarly in 1924, when the Democratic presidential candidate secured only a quarter of the state's vote, the party's senatorial candidate, an Irish-American, captured almost half the vote. In New York State, Al Smith was defeated for re-election as governor in 1920 by less than one hundred thousand votes, while Harding's majority over Cox was over one million; two years later Smith was returned as governor with the largest majority in the history of New York's gubernatorial races.

The results of these state contests suggest that despite the scrambled results of the 1920 and 1924 presidential contests, the traditional links between religion, ethnic group membership, class, and party support actually continued.

The story of the 1928 election, in which Al Smith ran as the first Catholic to hold the presidential nomination of a major party, has been told and analyzed by many. In this election, which aroused strong emotions and prejudices around the related issues of attitudes to Catholicism and Prohibition, the Smith campaign activated the poor, Catholic, Jewish, urban, immigrant groups, and alienated the small-town and rural native Protestants. Lubell has argued that a profound "social upheaval stirred beneath the Smith vote. What Smith really embodied was the revolt of the underdog urban immigrant against the top dog of 'Old American' stock. His Catholicism was an essential element in that revolt."[23]

The election of 1928 played a major role in structuring the subsequent alignment of American voters. It clearly

[23] Lubell, op. cit., pp. 37, 41.

brought to the national Democratic party all of the immigrant, Catholic, and Jewish vote which it had lost after World War I—and then some. Although many contemporaries blamed Smith's defeat on the success of a bitterly anti-Catholic campaign waged by the Ku Klux Klan and by many Protestant churchmen, the evidence does not sustain this thesis. In fact, Smith secured 41 per cent of the national vote, more than any other previous Democratic candidate in the twentieth century, except for Wilson running for re-election in 1916. It is likely that, as in the case of John F. Kennedy, thirty-two years later, Smith's religion won him more votes among coreligionists and other opponents of the Protestant Yankee Establishment than it lost him. Given the fact that the country was still in the midst of its greatest prosperity in history, Smith's ability to increase Democratic strength in the cities and much of the North, may be perceived as an indicator of the decline of both prohibitionist and anti-Catholic sentiment.

In 1932, Roosevelt retained the Catholic-Jewish and recent immigrant vote that had voted for Smith, and, of course, secured a considerable body of votes from other groups as a result of the reactions to the Great Depression.

From 1936 on, however, a more reliable measure of the correlates of vote decision exist, the data from public opinion surveys. Using such materials, it is possible to analyze the relative contribution of class as distinct from religious factors, such as the variations among different denominations and so forth.

Table 1 analyzes public opinion materials for each presidential election from 1936 to 1960, plus the congressional races of 1954 and 1956.

Southerners and Negroes have been excluded from tables because some of the relations we are concerned with are different among them. Negroes, though predominantly Protestant, have voted overwhelmingly Democratic since 1936. Southerners, ironically, continue their post-Civil War pattern of voting Democratic though this traditional loyalty has greatly declined in presidential contests.

Comparing the internal variations within the Protestant and Catholic groups, it seems evident that the pattern described for much of the nineteenth century has continued during the past twenty-four years. Class factors consistently differentiate among Protestants. That is, the middle-class Protestants have always been much more likely to back the Republicans than manual workers with similar religious loyalties. Among Catholics, however, class differences in party support, while present, are somewhat less powerful. Alford, who reports similar findings in his analysis of survey data from 1944 to 1960 (including Negroes and Southerners) comments that the lesser strength of the class-party relationship among Catholics is "consistent with the presumed ethnic and minority sentiments among Catholics which override class sentiments as a basis for political loyalties."[24] As "out-group" minorities, Catholics, Jews, and Negroes are much more likely to respond politically in terms of their ethnic-religious group identification than should the majority white Protestant population.

An examination of the data presented in Table 1 does suggest that the Catholic-Protestant difference has been somewhat more important than the manual-non-manual cleavage from 1936 to 1960. However when the impact of class is estimated by dividing the population into more classes, e.g., upper, upper-middle, middle, upper-lower, and lower or in terms of a number of occupational classes, e.g., large business, free professionals, down to unskilled workers, the variations linked to class become much greater. Well-to-do businessmen often vote from 80 to 90 per cent Republican, while semi-skilled and unskilled workers who are union members will vote 75 per cent Democratic."[25] Such differences are clearly larger than the variations between Catholics and Protestants. Similarly,

[24] Robert Alford, *Class Voting in Four Anglo-American Countries* (Ph.D. dissertation, University of California, Berkeley, 1961), p. 255.

[25] S. M. Lipset, *Political Man* (Garden City: Doubleday Anchor Books, 1963), pp. 303–306; and Harold Sheppard, Arthur Kornhauser, and Arthur Mayer, *When Labor Votes* (New York University Books, 1956), pp. 42–43.

TABLE 1

PERCENT VOTING DEMOCRATIC AMONG PROTESTANTS AND CATHOLICS WITHIN FARM, MANUAL, AND NON-MANUAL OCCUPATIONS
(NON-SOUTHERN WHITES ONLY)

Occupations	Total	Catholics	Protestants	Religious Voting (Difference between Catholics and Protestants)
		1936		
Farm	53	56	46	plus 10
Manual	71	86	63	plus 23
Non-manual	47	71	34	plus 37
Class voting (Difference between manual & non-manual)	plus 24	plus 15	plus 29	
Total		76	45	plus 31
		1940		
Farm	47	56	47	plus 9
Manual	67	85	53	plus 32
Non-manual	44	62	32	plus 30
Class voting	plus 23	plus 23	plus 21	
Total	44	72	41	plus 31

TABLE 1 Continued

Occupations	Total	Catholics	Protestants	(Difference between Religious Voting Catholics and Protestants)
		1944		
Farm	39	61	36	plus 25
Manual	63	74	55	plus 19
Non-manual	43	60	31	plus 29
Class voting	plus 20	plus 14	plus 24	
Total		68	41	plus 27
		1948		
Farm	48	62	47	plus 15
Manual	64	75	57	plus 18
Non-manual	46	59	35	plus 24
Class voting	plus 18	plus 16	plus 22	
Total		65	45	plus 20
		1952		
Farm	32	36	31	plus 5
Manual	52	63	43	plus 20
Non-manual	28	35	18	plus 17
Class voting	plus 24	plus 28	plus 25	
Total		32	30	plus 22

		1954		
Farm	38	33	38	less 5
Manual	62	74	54	plus 20
Non-manual	45	57	36	plus 21
Class voting	plus 17	plus 17	plus 18	plus 20
Total		64	44	

		1956		
Farm	45	78	39	plus 39
Manual	50	60	44	plus 16
Non-manual	33	49	21	plus 28
Class voting	plus 17	plus 11	plus 23	plus 22
Total		57	35	

		1958		
Farm	55	67	53	plus 14
Manual	66	59	57	plus 24
Non-manual	48	59	35	plus 24
Class voting	plus 18	plus 22	plus 22	plus 24
Total		71	47	

TABLE 1 Continued

Occupations	Total	Catholics 1960	Protestants	(Difference between Religious Voting Catholics and Protestants)
Farm	36	69	32	plus 37
Manual	58	84	43	plus 41
Non-manual	40	78	19	plus 59
Class voting	plus 18	plus 6	plus 24	
Total		81	33	plus 48

SOURCES: 1936—A.I.P.O. (Gallup Poll #141; 1940—A.I.P.O. #248; 1944—A.I.P.O. #323K; 1948—A.I.P.O. #454K; 1952—Michigan (Survey Research Center) Election Study, 1952; 1954—A.I.P.O. #539K; 1956—A.I.P.O. #573K; 1958—A.I.P.O. #608K; 1960—A.I.P.O. #638K.

In using the 1936 sample, it was necessary to define farmers as persons living on farms but not possessing manual or non-manual jobs.

In using the 1952 sample, it was necessary to define farmers as farm owners. Four states on the North-South border had to be excluded from this sample, but were included in the others.

the impact of religious affiliations on voting varies with degree of involvement in religious activities. Although the relationship differs with degree of commitment—the more religious members of a group are more likely to follow the dominant tendency of the group than the less religious or the irreligious—a correlation between voting and religion is not intensified as consistently or to the degree that occurs with the increased specification of class.

TABLE 2

RELATIONSHIP BETWEEN SOCIOECONOMIC STATUS AND TRADITIONAL PARTY PREFERENCE FOR THE THREE MAJOR RELIGIOUS GROUPINGS PER CENT DEMOCRATIC AND REPUBLICAN—1954

(WHITE RESPONDENTS ONLY)

Stratum	Protestant		Catholic		Jews	
	Dem.	Rep.	Dem.	Rep.	Dem.	Rep.
Non-manual						
Upper	14	61	36	39	31	0
Upper-Middle	24	49	36	27	55	10
Lower-Middle	25	44	50	18	63	5
Lower	45	40	64	7	x	x
Manual						
Upper-Middle	36	37	49	10	x	x
Lower-Middle	40	30	63	11	66	2
Lower	50	24	69	10	x	x
Farm						
Upper	24	41	x	x	x	x
Upper-Middle	29	44	38	44	x	x
Lower-Middle	32	43	58	20	x	x
Lower	34	41	44	12	x	x

SOURCE: Computed from the data of a survey conducted in eleven states by International Research Associates in 1954. The states are California, Michigan, Minnesota, Massachusetts, Iowa, New Mexico, Illinois, Ohio, Oregon, Pennsylvania, and New Jersey. Independents are not reported but are included in the base.

Some estimate of the effect of these factors may be seen in the statistics reported in Table 2 drawn from an analysis of a large opinion survey. Completed in 1954 it is based on a sample of 9852 interviews in 11 states outside of the South. With a sample of this magnitude, it is possible to examine the variation among a large number of classes within each major religious grouping.

An examination of Table 2 suggests that there is somewhat more variation within each religious group between the highest and lowest class than between Protestants and Catholics in the same class. Thus Catholics vary between 36 per cent Democratic in sympathies among "upper-class" non-manuals to 69 per cent within the lower manual stratum, or a difference of 33 per cent. The corresponding difference among Protestants between the highest and the lowest group is 36 per cent. Within any one stratum, the largest variation in per cent Democratic between Catholics and Protestants is 25 per cent, but most intraclass differences are less.

The usual concentration on the Protestant-Catholic-Jewish trichotomy serves to conceal variations among the Protestant denominations. When these are separated, the available survey evidence would suggest that the average socioeconomic status of the members of a given denomination is an important determinant of the relative position of the denomination with respect to support of the two major parties. However, there is some evidence that Protestant denominational differences do exist which are independent of class position. A large national sample of the electorate interviewed in the spring of 1952 was asked which party respondents have most often favored between 1936 and 1952. When this sample was differentiated among those in manual and non-manual occupations, the data indicated that the two "lowest status" and most fundamentalist groups of Protestants, Baptists and those classified under the heading of "other Protestants," contained the smallest proportion of Republicans within the manual and the non-manual strata. Conversely, the denominations of the more well-to-do, the Episcopalians, the Presbyterians, and the Congregationalists, contributed heavily to Republican support. A substantial majority of the manual workers who adhered to the latter groups indicated they had voted Republican most of the time. Lutherans seemed more Republican than one might have predicted from knowledge of their socio-economic position, while Methodists fell in a middle position with respect to Republican propensities.

These findings would suggest that worker members of predominantly high-status churches are greatly affected by the model opinion of the group, or perhaps, that the workers who adhere to such denominations do so in part because they are "upward mobile," that they seek to identify with the more privileged classes. Conversely, working-class members of the three lowest-status (in terms of average socioeconomic position) churches, the Baptists, the Methodists, and the Lutherans, are much more likely to be Democrats. The poorest denomination, the Baptists, are the most Democratic of all the major sects.

Benton Johnson offers an explanation of the seeming paradox that the more fundamentalist and ascetic Protestant groups are disproportionately Democratic. He first points to another paradox, that the churches of the more well-to-do have also been more liberal not only in their theology but in their social and economic pronouncements. The liberal National Council of Churches, though representing the wealthier Protestant denominations, has given considerable support to the Social Gospel movement. An analysis of the highest-status church in the United States, the Episcopal Church, based on questionnaire data from clergy and laymen, demonstrates convincingly that the clergy of this predominantly well-to-do denomination, are very liberal in their political views. On the other hand, the churches of the poorer Protestants, predominantly the Baptists and the smaller but numerous fundamentalist groups, have on the whole opposed the Social Gospel, and have taken conservative positions on economic and political issues.

Johnson argues that the political position of these groups are congruent with historic theological elements in ascetic Protestantism. The liberalism of the churches of the more well-to-do derive from the fact that their ministers are often men "who have received their training from the

more influential and prestigeful seminaries . . . many of
which are close to large universities, [and] have participated in the trend toward liberal humanitarianism that has
been going on in intellectual circles for many years."[26] The
churches of the poor, on the other hand, prefer a simple
unintellectual theology which defines Christianity in traditional terms, and preaches good versus evil, God against
Satan. Both parishioners and clergy tend to be low in
educational attainments, and the seminaries of these
groups are often deliberately removed from contact with
secular university life.

The fact that there is a general correlation between the
average socioeconomic status of the members of different
denominations and the religious and political liberalism
of their clergy and official church bodies suggests the
hypothesis that the more integrated an individual is in the
religious life of the liberal high-status churches, the more
liberal he should be in his outlook, holding other factors
constant; conversely the opposite pattern should occur
among the adherents of the low-status and more fundamentalist sects.

An analysis of interviews drawn from one city, Eugene,
Oregon, sustains these assumptions. As in the national data
presented above, members of low-status Eugene churches
are more likely to be Democrats than those adhering to
the high-status ones. These tendencies hold up within
classes as well. Manual workers and those in non-manual
occupations belonging to fundamentalist groups are more
Democratic than those in the same class adhering to the
liberal denominations. However, when the supporters of
the liberal churches are divided on the basis of church
attendance, frequent churchgoers show a lower Republican propensity than do those who go rarely. Among the
fundamentalist groups, the exact opposite occurs; frequent
attenders are more likely to vote Republican, while those

[26] Benton Johnson, "Ascetic Protestantism and Political
Preference," Public Opinion Quarterly 26, 1962, p. 39. Johnson,
op. cit., p. 39; for an analysis of the sources of the liberalism
of American academics and other intellectuals, see Lipset,
Political Man, op. cit., pp. 332–371.

who are rarely seen in church retain a strong Democratic alliance. This relationship holds up even when class position is held constant.

The finding that adherents of different denominations are disposed to follow the predominant political choice of the denomination may be shaped mainly by those who identify with, but are not involved in the religious life of a given church. To be a non-practicing Episcopalian or Congregationalist means to have a public high-status attribute; nominal church affiliation affects one's self-conception and public image, but apparently it does not much affect one's values. Hence non-practicing supporters of such churches are among the most Republican of individuals with comparable socioeconomic traits. Conversely, to remain identified with a low-status church means to retain a status ascribing characteristic that lowers one's general social status. An individual who so defines himself is presumably less oriented towards upward mobility, towards the values of the higher status groups. Consequently such people are among the most prone to vote Democratic within their stratum.

Religion, therefore, would seem to affect political choice in two independent ways, as a source of beliefs and as a determinant of status. And the two variables operate at cross purposes among Protestants. Active membership in a liberal high-status church pulls one towards political liberalism; nominal adherence primarily serves as a source of status and hence strengthens the political conservatism associated with high position. And the opposite pattern operates among the inactive and active adherents of the more fundamentalist low status groupings.

Variant Religious Values

In addition to the various social and historical factors that have shaped the political identity of religious groups, there are very direct relationships between different religious beliefs and value systems, and different political tendencies. Such relationships may take two forms: (1) explicit religious formulations which carry with them political directives; and (2) the indirect effect of religious systems in creating the dispositional base for the acceptance of certain secular political ideologies.

The most obvious example of the first type are the encyclicals of the Roman Catholic pontiffs. The economic ideology expressed in many encyclicals, while anti-socialist, has tended to favor what has come to be known as the welfare state. Since Pope Leo XIII, the Catholic Church has condemned the exploitation of labor by business, and has urged state protection against the insecurities of old age, unemployment, and the like. The Popes have also favored trade unions. In large measure, the theology of the Catholic Church stemming from precapitalist feudal and aristocratic origins, has been against what it calls "materialistic socialism *and* capitalism." A linkage between papal social encyclicals and American Catholics was provided in the statements of the American bishops which called for the adoption of "welfare state" measures long before they had a serious chance of enactment. Thus the yearly statement of the American Catholic Bishops in 1917 advocated liberal economic measures which were not put into effect until the party of the Protestant majority was finally defeated in the 1930s. The bishops suggested a heavier graduated income tax, social security, unemployment insurance, and minimum wage legislation.

It should be recognized, however, that there has been considerable diversity of opinion among the Catholic clergy, even on church-related matters. For decades a divergence has been recognized between "conservative" and "liberal" persuasions on such questions as the wisdom of continuing the Index of Prohibited Books, the moral propriety of state-run schools, and participation in interfaith activities.

Among the laity, too, striking evidence of diversity can be found. Efforts by the Church have kept laws on the books forbidding private physicians from dispensing contraceptive information in two states, Massachusetts and Connecticut. Yet, when Gallup interviewers asked a national sample in 1943, "Would you like to see government health clinics furnish birth control information to married people who wish it?" fully 45 per cent of the Catholics questioned responded in the affirmative.[27]

It is impossible to know how much effect official church positions have had on the political behavior of Catholics in different countries. Practicing Catholics have covered the range of the political spectrum from left-wing socialism to fascism. Local bishops have interpreted official church dogma to justify support of almost every political ideology except communism. There can, however, be little doubt that these church pronouncements have had some effect given the authoritative aura of the Church. For example, the sympathy which Catholic doctrine has had for trade union objectives, as contrasted with the greater emphasis on individualism inherent in Protestantism may in some part explain why even non-union member middle-class Catholics are more supportive of union rights in this country.

Perhaps more important in their effect on politics and other areas of life than the directly political manifestos of religious leaders are the ways in which religious doctrines operate to predispose adherents to favor one secular pattern rather than another. Many observers, for example, have called attention to the processes through which Protestantism has contributed to individualism, self-reliance, feelings of personal responsibility for success and failure, and interpretation of social evils in terms of moral turpitude. Catholicism, on the other hand, has tended to stress community responsibility, and does not emphasize individual morality. Emile Durkheim has pointed out the link between the differing stresses inherent in Protestantism and Catholicism in relation to variation in suicide rates. Durkheim's thesis is that Protestants are more prone than Catholics to commit suicide, for, among other reasons, Protestantism places greater responsibility on individuals for the consequences of their actions.

Similarly, it may be suggested that the differences among American Protestants and Catholics in their reac-

[27] Source: A.I.P.O. Study No. 308 KT, 1943.

tion to the welfare state may flow from a more or less conscious rejection of reliance on organized social action and the welfare state among Protestants. Studies of the 1948 and 1952 American presidential elections indicated that Protestant Republicans were more opposed to social welfare measures than Catholic Republicans.[28] Even when moral matters rather than welfare measures are at issue, white Protestants are less likely to support state action than are Catholics. In a study of the influence of religion on behavior Gerhard Lenski found that Protestants who thought that certain behaviors, i.e., gambling, moderate drinking, Sunday business, were "always or usually wrong" were less likely than Catholics to favor legal suppression of the immoral practice.

SUMMARY NOTE

There is obviously no simple solution to the study of the "religious factor" in American politics. Much of its influence must be perceived as part of the total value system affecting everyone. As we have seen membership in the same denominations stimulated feeling for and against slavery before the Civil War. Today, Southern Negroes and whites adhere to the same denominations, both are largely Baptist and Methodist. Foreign Catholic observers have noted to their dissatisfaction that many American Catholics have taken over Protestant puritanical attitudes, that the American Catholic's tastes, and ideas on moral issues are colored by people around him, and thus he is more like an American Baptist or Presbyterian than, let us say, a Mexican or Italian Catholic. The problem which co-variation of diverse elements with religious poses for analysis was explicitly recognized by Alexis de Tocqueville when he attempted to make sense out of American political life in the 1830s:

[28] A. Campbell, et. al., "Political Issues and the Vote," November 1952, *American Political Sciences Review* 47, 1953, pp. 374–375.

There is in each religion a political doctrine which by affinity, is joined to it. This point is controvertible in the sense that where nothing interferes with this tendency, it surely shows itself. But it doesn't follow that it is impossible to separate religious doctrines from their political effects. On the contrary, in all the countries of the world, material interests have been seen to operate this separation. The Catholics in . . . the United States are the invariable supporters of the "democratic" party. Does it follow that Catholicism leads to the "democratic" spirit? No, but that the Catholics are poor, and come almost all from a country where the aristocracy is Protestant.[29]

The combination of the "political doctrine" which, as Tocqueville suggests, is inherent in every religion with the fact that denominations in pluralistic America are variously located in the social and economic structure, and the continuing strong sense of commitment to an identification with religion means that religion remains, today, as in Tocqueville's time, one of the main sources of party cleavage and of political tone.

[29] Citation from Tocqueville's American diary as quoted in George W. Pierson, *Tocqueville in America* (Garden City: Doubleday Anchor Books, 1959), p. 289. He makes the same point with less stress on the problem of methodology in the *Democracy* itself. "Most of the Catholics are poor and they have no chance of taking part in the government unless it is open to all the citizens. They constitute a minority, and all rights must be respected in order to ensure to them the free exercise of their own privileges. These two causes induce them, even unconsciously, to adopt political doctrines which they would perhaps support with less zeal if they were rich and preponderant." Alexis de Tocqueville, op. cit., p. 312.

SOCIAL CLEAVAGE AND
RELIGIOUS CONFLICT

James S. Coleman

SOURCES OF SOCIAL CONFLICT

Consensus and Cleavage in Society

Cleavage between groups is in many respects only the obverse of consensus within groups. When people feel strong identification with a particular group, whether it is national, religious, ethnic, or another, they are necessarily setting themselves off from persons not in the group.

The analysis of social controversy, then, is not so much an analysis of *why* there is cleavage between groups, but a study of *which* groups are the foci of consensus and cleavage. It is like the problem of locating walls in a house: it is not a question of whether there will be walls to delineate rooms but rather a question of how the walls will be located, and what consequences a particular location will have for living convenience.

Thus the interesting question becomes this one: What are the different consequences of the lines of cleavage in society running one way rather than another? What are the consequences, for example, of having the primary psychological attachments being to national groups rather than religious groups? Or to local communities rather than a national community? Or to race rather than social class?

Suppose that social class overrode race as a boundary between groups in the United States, as it does in some European countries. Then since class carries no ineradicable distinguishing marks as does race, a man could move from stratum to stratum in an anonymous society like ours.

It would be impossible to classify a man irrevocably, as a Negro is classified by his skin color, and thus impossible to deny him the potentiality of society's highest rewards.

More generally, the consequences stem from this one question: When a crucial choice exists, when the issues are clear, then how are men going to line up: Which attachments are going to come to the fore and delineate the lines of cleavage? A man has many roles, and the crucial question is which of them dominates in a situation where they lead to different paths of action. The one underlying reason why interreligious conflict has been so important through the ages is that religious attachments have been among the most powerful men can feel. Only insofar as religion comes to play a lesser role in men's lives can the potential for religious conflict become weaker. This does not mean, of course, that the level of conflict between religious groups is fixed and invariant whenever the importance of religion in men's lives is fixed. Many other factors play a part; but insofar as religion is important to men, it constitutes the *potential* battle lines along which men may divide when conditions are right.

Lines of Cleavage and Levels of Conflict

Perhaps the most important variable having to do with the location of lines of social cleavage is the level at which these lines crosscut society. Major lines of cleavage may come *within* individuals or *between* individuals. If the lines of cleavage come within the individual, this is tantamount to saying that numerous roles are important to him, and that he will feel cross-pressures when faced with an issue—such as, for example, the issue of released time from public schools for religious instruction. The cross-pressured man is the man whose attachments lead him in both directions at once: to side with his religious beliefs, and to side with his attachments to secular public education.

The question is, what makes for or against cross-pressures? What brings the lines of cleavage within individuals or keeps them between individuals? The answer is simple: cross-pressures are absent when the major meaningful kinds of classification in society coincide. When such important lines of potential cleavage as ethnicity and religion and social status coincide, then there are few cross-pressures. That is, when Catholics are mostly Irish or Italian and mostly working class, while Protestants are mostly nth generation Americans of English and middle European backgrounds, and are white-collar workers or farmers, then the potential lines of cleavage in society coincide, and reduce the possibility of cross-pressures within individuals.

Group conflicts are at their strongest, are most likely to develop and least easily dissipated, when no conflict is felt within the person. This is one reason that conflicts between religious groups, as conflicts between national groups, have often been of considerable intensity. Members of a religious group feel little cross-pressure when faced with a conflict between their religious group and another. In contrast, conflicts between a religious group and the secular society comprised primarily of the same persons have been less strong. And least intense, in terms of the actual tactics of combat, has been the conflict within a religious group like the Catholic Church, resulting in the splitting off of fragmentary groups. It is only after a splinter group has irrevocably cut the bonds, so that such internal cross-pressures no longer exist, that these conflicts reach the intensity of interreligious conflicts. Martin Luther, for example, until his unequivocal break with the Church used tactics completely different from and much milder than those used when the conflict is between discrete religious groups.

When men are cross-pressured, they characteristically take one of several alternatives: they withdraw from the controversy, they delay taking sides, they attempt to keep others to whom they are attached out of the conflict, they maintain a low intensity of feeling toward either side. But one response is to take one side or the other. When this occurs, as it does initially when the conflict is between men who feel no cross-pressures, then a whole new set of responses occur. Men attempt to influence others who are uncommitted, they break off attachments which are inconsistent with their position, they change from mere disagreement with the other side to direct antagonism toward it, they invent new and diverse issues with which to gain new adherents and reinforce their position. This set of responses closely corresponds to the well-known "runaway" or "explosive" nature of conflict. When such responses exist among large numbers of people, that is, when large numbers of people are not at all cross-pressured, then the conflict takes on this explosive character, and can no longer be contained.

When one looks at the potential for cross-pressures in our society between religious attachments and others, interesting changes are evident. The economic, ethnic, and other groups which have paralleled religious groupings in the past are coming to cross-cut them now: Catholics have diffused upwards in the economic structure, and outward geographically to the suburbs; Jews similarly are less concentrated in particular economic roles and geographic locations than before; Protestants who grew up in one sect in a community are dispersed and recongregated in communities where sects must combine to survive. In sum, economic and geographic mobility is imposing new conditions of association and group identification on persons of different religious groups. These conditions will not break down religious cleavages; to the contrary, they may sometimes thrust together in a single community a combination of religious groups which makes for conflict; yet this dispersion has its effect in many ways; certainly by increasing the possibilities of cross-pressure; perhaps by bringing religious conflict more often to the community level, perhaps by reducing the intergroup suspicion and hostility which feed on dissociation; perhaps by initial disputes followed by gradual reduction of tensions.

Lines of Cleavage and the Size of Minority Groups

The history of religious restrictions in civil law in this country is suggestive concerning the effects of minority size. When the colonies were religiously homogeneous without any organized minority in the earliest days, religious restrictions in civil laws were great, and religious conflict took the form of persecution. Yet from the early nineteenth century until the early twentieth century, as religious diversity increased with immigration and mobility within the country, these restrictions were broken down. For example, laws requiring Bible reading in school were prevalent at the end of the eighteenth century. Yet few were added after that time, and from then until about 1913 there was a continual reduction in such laws. It appears that organized minority groups, Catholics, Jews, and different Protestant sects, in areas which had once been religiously homogeneous, easily broke down such laws through court action. Without such an organized opposition a religiously homogeneous community could maintain laws restricting religious liberty in violation of the constitution; but once organized minorities *did* exist, then restrictions were easily overcome.

However since 1913, and despite some Supreme Court decisions, there has been a growth of local and state laws compelling Bible reading in the classroom, released time for religious instruction, and similar measures reaffiliating religious and secular education. The reason for this is obscure, but one possibility is this: minority religions, particularly the Catholic Church, which once opposed an affiliation of religion and education because this threatened their existence, have now become well-established and powerful enough so that, rather than being threatened by such an affiliation, they are aided by it. Thus the very minority religious groups which once opposed such measures now support them, merely as a consequence of a shift in size and security.

Other examples of the effect of minority size on the group's response are abundant. Jews in the Bronx, surrounded by a majority of Jews, behave differently from Jews in the Midwest, surrounded by a majority of Protestants. And Protestants in the South, with few Catholics around them, behave differently in voting than do Protestants in the North, where Catholics are politically important. Southern Protestants shifted their votes in record numbers to defeat Alfred E. Smith for President; yet Protestants in the North who were Democratic, with Catholics dispersed among them not only geographically but socially as well, and in their party organizations, failed to turn against Al Smith to the same extent as did their colleagues in the South. Yet such a reaction might not have occurred; the existence of a deviant minority within a group often makes the group *more* cohesive than it would otherwise be, while this example suggests the opposite. Little is known systematically about the effect of the size of minorities on the behavior of the minority group and the majority group members.

INTRINSIC SOURCES OF RELIGIOUS CONFLICT

The paragraphs above have discussed some of the propositions which arise from a general study of social conflict. But there are certain peculiarities of religion which make it particularly susceptible to conflict, whether it be interreligious, intrareligious, or between a religious group and the state.

The Private Nature of Religious Experience

Much has been made by social scientists of the organized, institutional character of religion. But religious experience is also a mystical, private thing, a relation between a man and his God. Sometimes, as in Protestantism, this individual, private nature of religion is carried to the extreme. Yet Catholicism and Judaism, even with all their institutional aspects, have nearly as important a private meditative character as well. One consequence of this "communication with God" is that every man who so indulges is in communication with a different "person outside society," a person he has in part shaped with his own thoughts. That is, whenever a mystic or a monk or a devout believer engages in meditation and interpretation of the scripture, he can create a new creed. This possibility poses a constant threat of cleavage within a religious group. The very nature of religion itself as a mystical experience offers the constant potential for a new revelation, and with it a new set of beliefs. The path is always open for a revelation from God, establishing a new sect at odds with those around it. Nothing more may be required than a man who is ambitious or who seeks to "discover God for himself," and who has the necessary leadership qualities.

The divisive potential of such a situation is reflected by the Catholic Church's strict ban on freethinking, its insistence on the Pope as mediator between man and his God, in order to interpret the scriptures aright to him. In fact, the institution of confessionals in the Church could hardly be better designed to undermine the potential for cleavage. The priest (a member of the hierarchy and thus himself subject to discipline for possible deviation) is the mediator who insures that the "word of God" which a supplicant hears is always the same word, and can be depended upon not to lead a follower into deviant paths. Yet even with such stringent restrictions built into the religious creed, deviations within the Church continue to arise from the personal inner-experience character of religion. The tradition of miracles and sainthood constitutes one of the Church's means of coping with mystics; but saints have always been a problem for the Church, arising as they do outside the hierarchy of established religious authority.

Religion as a Source of Alternative Values

A further basis for religious conflict—this time conflict between religious and secular society, or between different religions—is perhaps even more fundamental, for it derives from the function which religion has always performed for poor, oppressed, or unhappy people. It was Karl Marx who pointed out that religion acted as an opiate of the masses to divert them from pure class consciousness and from their struggle for a classless society. This is simply another way of saying that religion serves a peculiar and important function for the oppressed and the poor in society: it provides them with a hope and belief that sometime, somewhere, there will be a different set of values by which status is derived, a set of values which will make them the "chosen people" or those who "inherit the earth."

When religion tells the oppressed and burdened that *they* are the chosen people, or that *they* are among the select few who will pass through the gates of heaven, religion thereby gives them a release from the values of a society which locates them so low in the eyes of themselves and others. Though their religious creed seldom dictates that they actively rebel against others (an exception is the Hebrew religion which brought the Jews out of Egypt), it provides the potentialities for such rebellion simply by telling each religious group that they are superior. To be sure, it may comfort them so that they are pacified, and need not revolt or work to gain prestige in the eyes of the rest of society; but without such an alternative set of values which religion provides (or which, it may be noted, a socialist ideology also provides), they would not even have the psychological basis for rebellion or other activity. A belief in religion thus acts just as does a deviant political ideology in freeing men from the value constraints imposed by society. If they were forced to hold these accepted social values and no others, a psychological equilibrium would hardly be possible for the poor and oppressed. Religious values, in helping maintain such an equilibrium, also provide the possibility of cleavage, division, and ultimately conflict.

Examples are abundant of religious belief serving as the basis for conflict stemming from a rejection of socially accepted values. The escape of the Jews from Egypt, the Crusades, and Gandhi's non-violent resistance movement, predicated on religion, are three important cases; though in all of these cases other factors such as nationalism and ethnicity added fuel to the flames started by religion.

One of the most important derivatives of religion's "alternative-value" function is the establishment of strong in-group feelings. Particularly if the group is small, such feelings are necessary if the group members are to maintain their alternative values in a hostile or indifferent environment; but in turn such feelings are further generated by these values, which emphasize the goodness of one's fellow-members. Each religious sect is, in a sense, a mutual admiration society.

Feelings of group identity of course help set the stage for conflict, for they establish a "we" and "they," and bring about an investment of the ego in the group. This ego-investment, in turn, means that all the defenses and needs of the ego are expanded to encompass the whole group. Whether a man is a Jehovah's Witness, a Jew, a Catholic, or a Presbyterian, a slight or insult to his religious group is a personal one, to be reacted to as a personal insult. It is obvious, then, that such group identification, derived in part from the alternative values which religion provides, creates a basis for conflict between religions or between a religious group and secular society.

The Genesis of Cleavage by Association and Dissociation

One fundamental social process which plays an important role in conflict between religious groups is the genesis of disagreement through dissociation. Catholics associate with Catholics, Jews with Jews, and Protestants with Protestants. Now given that this is true (and numerous empirical studies have shown that religion is as important a basis of association in our society as any other except race), numerous consequences follow. The process through which dissociation leads to disagreement is one of the most important. Socio-psychological mechanisms come into play to create suspicion, hostility, and fear within each group that is socially isolated from another. An account of a community conflict in the twenties between Presbyterians and Methodists in the same community illustrates these processes well:

In a small farming community of the Northeast, there had been intense rivalry between the churches. The Presbyterians of the early days are said to have been

of an unusually "Blue" variety. They called the Methodists "howling Methodists." The school was near
the Methodist Church, and some of the parents would
warn their children not to pass this church in going
to school, lest they be contaminated by the Methodist
ideas.[1]

Similarly, a Catholic writes of his childhood as a Catholic
among Protestants:

> I began to hear what came to be familiar phrases:
> "those people," "the Prods," "our own kind," "they
> don't want us." I became aware that we did not live
> in a community of friendly neighbors, but that as
> Catholics we were camped instead in the middle of
> warlike Protestants.[2]

These accounts of dissociation coupled with feelings of
religious group identity illustrate how strongly reinforcing
these two elements are: *feeling* together and *associating*
together, or alternatively feeling apart from others and
associating apart from them. Religion has been so fully
tied to numerous other social institutions (ethnic groups,
nationality groups, economic groups, communities, and
such ancillary religious institutions as welfare organizations,
schools, youth groups, informal associations, and so on)
that it has been a major means by which boundaries of
association have been defined in society. As a consequence, religious groups have constituted closed "pockets"
within which opinions can resonate and values can evolve
in isolation from others.

Generational Transmission

Another source of religious conflict, obvious though it
may be, is nevertheless distinct from those that have gone
before. It is due to the fact that religion is usually a family
matter, transmitted from generation to generation as part

[1] The Inquiry, *Community Conflict.* New York: 1929, p. 119.
[2] Thomas Sugrue, *A Catholic Speaks His Mind on America's
Religious Conflict* (New York: Harper, 1951), p. 47.

of a general cultural heritage. Thus religious differences are built into children at an early age, either as direct transmission of values, or indirectly through their effect on child-rearing practices. Such differences have a double effect in creating diversity paralleling religion: they provide different sets of *values* from a very early age; but even more fundamentally, they create different *personalities*. A Baptist mother, a Catholic mother, and a Jewish mother bring up their children quite differently. It could almost be predicted that these children would fail to understand each other as adults, when their personality structures as well as their values differ.

In summary, the potential for social conflict exists by the very way in which people identify themselves with groups, forming lines of consensus and cleavage in society: but beyond this, the potential for religious conflict exists by virtue of the very functions which religion performs for people. For both these reasons, insofar as religion fulfills the same functions for people as it has in the past, it will be attended by intergroup diversity, conflict, and cleavage.

THE RELIGION OF AMERICANS AND AMERICAN RELIGION

Will Herberg

What do Americans believe? Most emphatically, they
"believe in God": 97 per cent according to one survey, 96
per cent according to another, 95 per cent according to a
third. About 75 per cent of them regard themselves as
members of churches, and a sizable proportion attend
divine services with some frequency and regularity. They
believe in prayer: about 90 per cent say they pray on
various occasions. They believe in life after death, even
in heaven and hell. They think well of the church and of
ministers. They hold the Bible to be an inspired book,
the "word of God." By a large majority they think children should be given religious instruction and raised as
church members. By a large majority, too, they hold religion to be of very great importance. In all of these respects
their attitudes are as religious as those of any people today,
or, for that matter, as those of any Western people in
recent history.

Yet these indications are after all relatively superficial;
they tell us what Americans say (and no doubt believe)
about themselves and their religious views; they do not
tell us what in actuality these religious views are. Nowhere are surface appearances more deceptive, nowhere
is it more necessary to try to penetrate beyond mere
assertions of belief than in such ultimate matters as religion.

The surveys reveal certain curious discrepancies in the
responses people make to questions about their religion.
Thus, according to one trustworthy source, 73 per cent
said they believed in an after life, with God as judge,
but "only 5 percent [had] any fear, not to say expecta-

tion, of going [to hell]." Indeed, about 80 per cent, according to another source, admitted that what they were "most serious about" was not the life after death in which they said they believed, but in trying to live as comfortably in this life as possible. And in their opinion they were not doing so badly even from the point of view of the divine judgment: 91 per cent felt that they could honestly say that they were trying to lead a good life, and 78 per cent felt no hesitation in saying that they more than half measured up to their own standards of goodness, over 50 per cent asserting that they were in fact following the rule of loving one's neighbor as oneself "all the way"! This amazing high valuation that most Americans appear to place on their own virtue would seem to offer a better insight into the basic religion of the American people than any figures as to their formal beliefs can provide, however important in themselves these figures may be.

But perhaps the most significant discrepancy in the assertions Americans make about their religious views is to be found in another area. When asked, "Would you say your religious beliefs have any effect on your ideas of politics and business?", a majority of the same Americans who had testified that they regarded religion as something "very important" answered that their religious beliefs had no real effect on their ideas or conduct in these decisive areas of everyday life; specifically, 54 per cent said no, 39 per cent said yes, and 7 per cent refused to reply or didn't know. This disconcerting confession of the irrelevance of religion to business and politics was attributed by those who appraised the results of the survey as pointing to a calamitous divorce between the "private" and the "public" realms in the religious thinking of Americans. There is certainly a great deal of truth in this opinion, and we shall have occasion to explore it in a different context, but in the present connection it would seem that another aspect of the matter is more immediately pertinent. Some ideas and standards undeniably govern the conduct of Americans in their affairs of business and politics; if they are not ideas and standards associated with the teachings of religion, what are they? It will not do to say that people just act "selfishly" without reference to moral standards of any kind. All people act "selfishly," of course; but it is no less true of all people, Americans included, that their "selfishness" is controlled, mitigated, or, at worst, justified by some sort of moral commitment, by some sort of belief in a system of values beyond immediate self-interest. The fact that more than half the people openly admit that their religious beliefs have no effect on their ideas of politics and business would seem to indicate very strongly that, over and above conventional religion, there is to be found among Americans some sort of faith or belief or set of convictions, not generally designated as religion but definitely operative as such in their lives in the sense of providing them with some fundamental context of normativity and meaning.

II

"Every functioning society," Robin M. Williams, Jr. points out, "has to an important degree a common religion. The possession of a common set of ideas, rituals, and symbols can supply an overarching sense of unity even in a society riddled with conflicts."[1] What is this "common religion" of American society, the "common set of ideas, rituals, and symbols" that give it its "overarching sense of unity"? Williams provides us with a further clue when he suggests that "men are always likely to be intolerant of opposition to their central ultimate values."[2] What are these "central ultimate values" about which Americans are "intolerant"? No one who knows anything about the religious situation in this country would be likely to suggest that the things Americans are "intolerant" about are the beliefs, standards, or teachings of the religions they "officially" acknowledge as theirs. Americans are proud of their tolerance in matters of religion: one is

[1] Robin M. Williams, *American Society: A Sociological Interpretation* (Knopf, 1951), p. 312.
[2] Ibid, pp. 32 ff.

expected to "believe in God," but otherwise religion is not supposed to be a ground of "discrimination." This is, no doubt, admirable, but is it not "at least in part, a sign that the crucial values of the system are no longer couched in a religious framework"?[3]

What, then, is the "framework" in which they *are* couched? What, to return to our original question, is the "common religion" of the American people, as it may be inferred not only from their words but also from their behavior?

It seems to me that a realistic appraisal of the values, ideas, and behavior of the American people leads to the conclusion that Americans, by and large, do have their "common religion" and that that "religion" is the system familiarly known as the American Way of Life. It is the American Way of Life that supplies American society with an "overarching sense of unity" amid conflict. It is the American Way of Life about which Americans are admittedly and unashamedly "intolerant." It is the American Way of Life that provides the framework in terms of which the crucial values of American existence are couched. By every realistic criterion the American Way of Life is the operative faith of the American people.

It would be the crudest kind of misunderstanding to dismiss the American Way of Life as no more than a political formula or propagandist slogan, or to regard it as simply an expression of the "materialistic," no doubt, but surely not more so than other people, than the French peasant or petty bourgeois, for example. All such labels are irrelevant, if not meaningless. The American Way of Life is, at bottom, a spiritual structure, a structure of ideas and ideals, of aspirations and values, of beliefs and standards; it synthesizes all that commends itself to the American as the right, the good, and the true in actual life. It embraces such seemingly incongruous elements as sanitary plumbing and freedom of opportunity, Coca-Cola and an intense faith in education—all felt as moral questions relating to the proper way of life. The very expression

[3] *Ibid.*, p. 344.

"way of life" points to its religious essence, for one's ultimate, over-all way of life is one's religion.

The American Way of Life is, of course, conceived as the corporate "way" of the American people, but it has its implications for the American as an individual as well. It is something really operative in his actual life. When in the *Ladies' Home Journal* poll, Americans were asked "to look within [themselves] and state honestly whether [they] thought [they] really obeyed the law of love under certain special conditions," 90 per cent said yes and 5 per cent no when the one to be "loved" was a person belonging to a different religion; 80 per cent said yes and 12 per cent no when it was the case of a member of a different race; 78 per cent said yes and 10 per cent no when it concerned a business competitor—but only 27 per cent said yes and 57 per cent no in the case of "a member of a political party that you think is dangerous," while 25 per cent said yes and 63 per cent said no when it concerned an enemy of the nation. These figures are most illuminating, first because of the incredible self-assurance they reveal with which the average American believes he fulfills the "impossible" law of love, but also because of the light they cast on the differential impact of the violation of this law on the American conscience. For it is obvious that the figures reflect not so much the actual behavior of the American people—no people on earth ever loved their neighbors as themselves as much as the American people say they do—as how seriously Americans take transgressions against the law of love in various cases. Americans feel they *ought* to love their fellow men despite differences of race or creed or business interest; that is what the American Way of Life emphatically prescribes. But the American Way of Life almost explicitly sanctions hating a member of a "dangerous" political party (the Communist party is obviously meant here) or an enemy of one's country, and therefore an overwhelming majority avow their hate. In both situations, while the Jewish-Christian law of love is formally acknowledged, the truly operative factor is the value system embodied in the American Way of Life. Where the American Way of Life approves of love of one's fellow man, most Americans confidently assert that they practice such love; where the American Way of Life disapproves, the great mass of Americans do not hesitate to confess that they do not practice it, and apparently feel very little guilt for their failure. No better pragmatic test as to what the operative religion of the American people actually is could be desired.

It is not suggested here that the ideals Americans feel to be indicated in the American Way of Life are scrupulously observed in the practice of Americans; they are in fact constantly violated, often grossly. But violated or not, they are felt to be normative and relevant to "business and politics" in a way that the formal tenets of "official" religion are not. That is what makes the American Way of Life the "common religion" of American society in the sense here intended.

It should be clear that what is being designated under the American Way of Life is not the so-called common denominator religion; it is not a synthetic system composed of beliefs to be found in all or a group of religions. It is an organic structure of ideas, values, and beliefs that constitutes a faith common to Americans and genuinely operative in their lives, a faith that markedly influences, and is influenced by, the "official" religions of American society. Sociologically, anthropologically, if one pleases, it is the characteristic American religion, undergirding American life and overarching American society despite all indubitable differences of region, section, culture, and class.

Yet qualifications are immediately in order. Not for all Americans is this American religion, this "common religion" of American society, equally operative; some indeed explicitly repudiate it as religion. By and large, it would seem that what is resistive in contemporary American society to the American Way of Life as religion may be understood under three heads. First, there are the churches of immigrant-ethnic background that still cherish their traditional creeds and confessions as a sign of their distinctive origin and are unwilling to let these be dissolved into an over-all "American religion"; certain Lutheran and Reformed churches in this country as well as sections of the Catholic Church would fall into this classification. Then there are groups, not large but increasing, that have an explicit and conscious theological concern, whether it be "orthodox," "neo-orthodox," or "liberal"; in varying degrees, they find their theologies at odds with the implied "theology" of the American Way of Life. Finally, there are the ill-defined, though by all accounts numerous and influential, "religions of the disinherited," the many "holiness," pentecostal, and millenarian sects of the socially and culturally submerged segments of our society; for them, their "peculiar" religion is frequently still too vital and all-absorbing to be easily subordinated to some "common faith." All of these cases, it will be noted, constitute "holdouts" against the sweep of religious Americanism; in each case there is an element of alienation which generates a certain amount of tension in social life.

What is this American Way of Life that we have said constitutes the "common religion" of American society? An adequate description and analysis of what is implied in this phrase still remains to be attempted, and certainly it will not be ventured here; but some indications may not be out of place.

The American Way of Life is the symbol by which Americans define themselves and establish their unity. German unity, it would seem, is felt to be largely racial-folkish, French unity largely cultural; but neither of these ways is open to the American people, the most diverse in racial and cultural origins of any in the world. As American unity has emerged, it has emerged more and more clearly as a unity embodied in, and symbolized by, the complex structure known as the American Way of Life.

If the American Way of Life had to be defined in one word, "democracy" would undoubtedly be the word, but democracy in a peculiarly American sense. On its political side it means the Constitution; on its economic side, "free enterprise"; on its social side, an equalitarianism which is not only compatible with but indeed actually implies vigorous economic competition and high mobility. Spiritually, the American Way of Life is best expressed in a certain kind of "idealism" which has come to be recognized as characteristically American. It is a faith that has its symbols and its rituals, its holidays and its liturgy, its saints and its sancta; and it is a faith that every American, to the degree that he is an American, knows and understands.

The American Way of Life is individualistic, dynamic, pragmatic. It affirms the supreme value and dignity of the individual; it stresses incessant activity on his part, for he is never to rest but is always to be striving to "get ahead"; it defines an ethic of self-reliance, merit, and character, and judges by achievement: "deeds, not creeds" are what count. The American Way of Life is humanitarian, "forward-looking," optimistic. Americans are easily the most generous and philanthropic people in the world, in terms of their ready and unstinting response to suffering anywhere on the globe. The American believes in progress, in self-improvement, and quite fanatically in education. But above all, the American is idealistic. Americans cannot go on making money or achieving worldly success simply on its own merits; such "materialistic" things must, in the American mind, be justified in "higher" terms, in terms of "service" or "stewardship" or "general welfare." Because Americans are so idealistic, they tend to confuse espousing an ideal with fulfilling it and are always tempted to regard themselves as good as the ideals they entertain: hence the amazingly high valuation most Americans quite sincerely place on their own virtue. And because they are so idealistic, Americans tend to be moralistic: they are inclined to see all issues as plain and simple, black and white, issues of morality. Every struggle in which they are seriously engaged becomes a "crusade." To Mr. Eisenhower, who in many ways exemplifies American religion in a particularly representative way, the Second World War was a "crusade" (as was the first to Woodrow Wilson); so was his campaign for the presidency ("I am engaged in a crusade . . . to substitute good government for what we most earnestly believe has been bad government"); and so is his administration—a "battle for the republic" against "godless Communism" abroad and against "corruption and materialism" at home. It was Woodrow Wilson who once said, "Sometimes people call me an idealist. Well, that is the way I know I'm an American: America is the most idealistic nation in the world"; Eisenhower was but saying the same thing when he solemnly affirmed: "The things that make us proud to be Americans are of the soul and of the spirit."[4]

The American Way of Life is, of course, anchored in the American's vision of America. The Puritan's dream of a new "Israel" and a new "Promised Land" in the New World, the "novus ordo seclorum" on the Great Seal of the United States reflect the perennial American conviction that in the New World a new beginning has been made, a new order of things established, vastly different from and superior to the decadent institutions of the Old World. This conviction, emerging out of the earliest reality of American history, was continuously nourished through the many decades of immigration into the present century by the residual hopes and expectations of the immigrants, for whom the New World had to be really something new if it was to be anything at all. And this conviction still remains pervasive in American life, hardly shaken by the new shape of the world and the challenge of the "new orders" of the twentieth century, nazism and communism. It is the secret of what outsiders must take to be the incredible self-righteousness of the American people, who tend to see the world divided into an innocent, virtuous America confronted with a corrupt, devious, and guileful Europe and Asia. The self-righteousness, however, if self-righteousness it be, is by no means simple, if only because virtually all Americans are themselves derived from the foreign parts they so distrust. In any case, this feeling about America as really and truly the "new order" of things at last established is the heart of the outlook defined by the American Way of Life.

In her *Vermont Tradition*, Dorothy Canfield Fisher lists

[4] For the quotations, as well as a general account of Mr. Eisenhower's religion, see Paul Hutchinson, "The President's Religious Faith," *The Christian Century*, March 24, 1954.

as that tradition's principal ingredients: individual freedom, personal independence, human dignity, community responsibility, social and political democracy, sincerity, restraint in outward conduct, and thrift.[5] With some amplification—particularly emphasis on the uniqueness of the American "order" and the great importance assigned to religion—this may be taken as a pretty fair summary of some of the "values" embodied in the American Way of Life. It will not escape the reader that this account is essentially an idealized description of the middle-class ethos. And, indeed, that is just what it is. The American Way of Life is a middle-class way, just as the American people in their entire outlook and feeling are a middle-class people. But the American Way of Life as it has come down to us is not merely middle-class; it is emphatically inner-directed. Indeed, it is probably one of the best expressions of inner-direction in history. As such, it now seems to be undergoing some degree of modification—perhaps at certain points disintegration—under the impact of the spread of other-direction in our society. For the foreseeable future, however, we may with some confidence expect the continuance in strength of the American Way of Life as both the tradition and the "common faith" of the American people.

III

The American Way of Life as the "common faith" of American society has coexisted for some centuries with the historic faiths of the American people, and the two have influenced each other in many profound and subtle ways. The influence has been complex and reciprocal, to the point where causal priority becomes impossible to assign if indeed it does not become altogether meaningless. From the very beginning the American Way of Life was shaped by the contours of American Protestantism; it may, indeed, best be understood as a kind of secularized Puri-

[5] Dorothy Canfield Fisher, *Vermont Tradition* (Boston: Little Brown, 1953).

tanism, a Puritanism without transcendence, without sense of sin or judgment. The Puritan's vision of a new "Promised Land" in the wilderness of the New World has become, as we have suggested, the American's deep sense of the newness and uniqueness of things in the Western Hemisphere. The Puritan's sense of vocation and "inner-worldly asceticism" can still be detected in the American's gospel of action and service, and his consciousness of high responsibility before God in the American's "idealism." The Puritan's abiding awareness of the ambiguity of all human motivations and his insight into the corruptions of inordinate power have left their mark not only on the basic structure of our constitutional system but also on the entire social philosophy of the American people. Nor have other strands of early American Protestantism been without their effect. There can be little doubt that pietism co-operated with frontier revivalism in breaking down the earlier concern with dogma and doctrine, so that the slogan "Deeds, not creeds" soon became the hallmark both of American religion and of the American Way of Life. These are but aspects of an influence that is often easier to see than to define.

The reciprocal action of the American Way of Life in shaping and reshaping the historic faiths of Christianity and Judaism on American soil is perhaps more readily discerned. By and large, we may say that these historic religions have all tended to become "Americanized" under the pervasive influence of the American environment. This "Americanization" has been the product not so much of conscious direction as of a "diffuse convergence" operating spontaneously in the context of the totality of American life. What it has brought, however, is none the less clear: "religious groupings throughout [American] society [have been] stamped with recognizably 'American' qualities," to an extent indeed where foreign observers sometimes find the various American religions more like each other than they are like their European counterparts.

American religion is (within the limits set by the particular traditions of the churches) non-theological and non-liturgical; it is activistic and occupied with the things of the world to a degree that has become a byword among European churchmen. With this activism has gone a certain "latitudinarianism," associated with the de-emphasis of theology and doctrine: Americans tend to believe that "ethical behavior and a good life, rather than adherence to a specific creed, (will) earn a share in the heavenly kingdom.[6] The activism of American religion has manifested itself in many forms throughout our history: in the Puritan concern for the total life of the community; in the passionate championing of all sorts of reform causes by the evangelical movements of the first half of the nineteenth century; in the "social gospel" of more recent times; in the ill-starred Prohibition "crusade"; in the advanced "progressive" attitudes on social questions taken by the National Council of Churches, the National Catholic Welfare Conference, and the various rabbinical associations; in the strong social emphasis of American Protestant "neo-orthodoxy." This activism, which many Europeans seem to regard as the distinguishing feature of American religion, both reflects the dynamic temper of the American Way of Life and has been a principal factor in its development.

Moreover, Americans believe in religion in a way that perhaps no other people do. It may indeed be said that the primary religious affirmation of the American people, in harmony with the American Way of Life, is that religion is a "good thing," a supremely "good thing," for the individual and the community. And "religion" here means not so much any particular religion, but religion as such. "Our government makes no sense," President Eisenhower recently declared, "unless it is founded in a deeply felt religious faith—*and I don't care what it is*" (emphasis added).[7] In saying this, the President was saying something that almost any American could understand and approve, but which must seem like a deplorable heresy

[6] Oscar Handlin, *The Uprooted* (Boston: Little, Brown, 1951), p. 128.

[7] New York *Times*, December 23, 1952; see also G. Elson Ruff, *The Dilemma of Church and State* (Muhlenberg, 1954), p. 85.

to the European churchman. Every American could understand, first, that Mr. Eisenhower's apparent indifferentism ("and I don't care what it is") was not indifferentism at all, but the expression of the conviction that at bottom the "three great faiths" were really "saying the same thing" in affirming the "spiritual ideals" and "moral values" of the American Way of Life. Every American, moreover, could understand that what Mr. Eisenhower was emphasizing so vehemently was the indispensability of religion as the foundation of society. This is one aspect of what Americans mean when they say that they "believe in religion." The object of devotion of this kind of religion, however, is "not God but 'religion'. . . . The faith is not in God but in faith; we worship not God but our own worshiping".[8] When Americans think of themselves as profoundly religious people whose "first allegiance" is "reserved . . . to the kingdom of the spirit,"[9] this is, by and large, what they mean, and not any commitment to the doctrines or traditions of the historic faiths.

With this view of religion is associated a closely analogous view of the church. For America, the celebrated dichotomy of "church" and "sect," however pertinent it may be to European conditions, has only a secondary significance. The concept of the church as the nation religiously organized, established socially, if not always legally, has no relevance whatever to American reality; and though America does know sects in the sense of "fringe" groups of the "disinherited," it does not understand these groups and their relation to the more conventional churches the way Europe does. An entirely new conception of church and church institutions has emerged in America.

It must be remembered that in America the variety and multiplicity of churches did not, as in Europe, come with the breakdown of a single established national church;

[8] Miller, "Piety Along the Potomac," *The Reporter,* August 17.

[9] Dwight D. Eisenhower, quoted in Paul Hutchinson, "The President's Religious Faith," *The Christian Century,* March 24, 1954.

in America, taking the nation as a whole, the variety and multiplicity of churches was almost the original condition and coeval with the emergence of the new society. In America, religious pluralism is thus not merely a historical and political fact; it is, in the mind of the American, the primordial condition of things, an essential aspect of the American Way of Life, and therefore in itself an aspect of religious belief. Americans, in other words, believe that the plurality of religious groups is a proper and legitimate condition. However much he may be attached to his own church, however dimly he may regard the beliefs and practices of other churches, the American tends to feel rather strongly that total religious uniformity, even with his own church benefiting thereby, would be something undesirable and wrong, indeed scarcely conceivable. Pluralism of religions and churches is something quite axiomatic to the American. This feeling, more than anything else, is the foundation of the American doctrine of the "separation of church and state," for it is the heart of this doctrine that the government may not do anything that implies the pre-eminence or superior legitimacy of one church over another.

This means that outside the Old World distinction of church and sect America has given birth to a new type of religious structure—the denomination. The denomination as we know it is a stable settled church, enjoying a legitimate and recognized place in a larger aggregate of churches, each recognizing the proper status of the others. The denomination is the "non-conformist sect" become central and normative. It differs from the church in the European understanding of the term in that it would never dream of claiming to be *the* national ecclesiastical institution; it differs from the sect in that it is socially established, thoroughly institutionalized, and nuclear to the society in which it is found. The European dichotomy becomes meaningless, and instead we have the nuclear denomination on the one side, and the peripheral sect on the way to becoming a denomination on the other. So firmly entrenched is this denominational idea in the mind of the American that even American Catholics have come to think in such terms; theologically the Catholic Church of course continues to regard itself as the one true church, but in their actual social attitudes American Catholics, hardly less than American Protestants or Jews, tend to think of their church as a denomination existing side by side with other denominations in a pluralistic harmony that is felt to be somehow of the texture of American life.

The denominational idea is fundamental to American thinking about religion, but it is not the last word. Americans think of their various churches as denominations, but they also feel that somehow the denominations fall into larger wholes which we have called religious communities. This kind of denominational aggregation is, of course, something that pertains primarily to Protestantism and to a lesser degree to Judaism; both have more or less organized denominations which, taken together, form the religious communities. Catholicism, on the other hand, has no such overt inner divisions, but American Catholics readily understand the phenomenon when they see it among Protestants and Jews. Denominations are felt to be somehow a matter of individual preference, and movement between denominations is not uncommon; the religious community, on the other hand, is taken as something more objective and given, something in which, by and large, one is born, lives, and dies, something that identifies and defines one's position in American society.

When the plurality of denominations comprehended in religious communities is seen from the standpoint of the "common faith" of American society, what emerges is the conception of the three "communions"—Protestantism, Catholicism, Judaism—as three diverse, but equally legitimate, equally American, expressions of an over-all American religion, standing for essentially the same "moral ideals" and "spiritual values." This conception, whatever may be thought of it theologically, is in fact held, though hardly in explicit form, by many devout and religiously sophisticated Americans. It would seem to be the obvious meaning of the title "The Religions of Democracy," given to a recent authoritative statement of the Protestant, Catholic, and Jewish positions.[10] "Democracy" apparently has its religions which fall under it as species fall under the genus of which they are part. And in this usage "democracy" is obviously a synonym for the American Way of Life.

It is but one more step, though a most fateful one, to proceed from "the religions of democracy" to "democracy as religion" and consciously to erect "democracy" into a super-faith above and embracing the three recognized religions. This step has been taken by a number of thinkers in recent years. Thus, Professor J. Paul Williams has been urging a program of religious reconstruction in which he insists that: "Americans must come to look on the democratic ideal (not necessarily the American practice of it) as the Will of God, or if they please, of Nature . . . Americans must be brought to the conviction that democracy is the very Law of Life . . . The state must be brought into the picture; governmental agencies must teach the democratic ideal *as religion* . . . primary responsibility for teaching democracy as religion must be given to the public school, for instance . . ."[11]

Professor Horace M. Kallen reaches very much the same conclusion from another direction. "For the communicants of the democratic faith," he writes, "it is the religion *of* and *for* religions. . . . [It is] the religion, all may freely come together in it."[12]

This marks a radical break with the fundamental presuppositions of both Judaism and Christianity, to which it must appear as a particularly insidious kind of idolatry. What is merely implicit and perhaps never intended in the acceptance of the American Way of Life as the "common

[10] Louis Finkelstein, J. Elliott Ross, and William Adams Brown, *The Religions of Democracy: Judaism, Catholicism, and Protestantism in Creed and Life* (New York: Devin-Adair, 1946).

[11] J. Paul Williams, *What Americans Believe and How They Worship* (Harper, 1952), pp. 71, 78, 368, 374.

[12] H. M. Kallen, "Democracy's True Religion," *Saturday Review of Literature*, July 28, 1951.

religion" of American society is here brought to its logical conclusion and made to reveal its true inner meaning.

By and large, the "common faith" of American society remains implicit and is never carried to the logical conclusion to which a few ideologists have pushed it. By the great mass of the American people the American Way of Life is not avowed as a super-faith above and embracing the historic religions. It operates as a "common faith" at deeper levels, through its pervasive influence on the patterns of American thought and feeling. It makes no pretensions to override or supplant the recognized religions, to which it assigns a place of great eminence and honor in the American scheme of things. But all the implications are there. . . .

IV

The "common faith" of American society is not merely a civic religion to celebrate the values and convictions of the American people as a corporate entity. It has its inner, personal aspects as well; or rather, side by side and in intimate relation with the civic religion of the American Way of Life, there has developed, primarily through a devitalization of the historic faiths, an inner, personal religion that promises salvation to the disoriented, tormented souls of a society in crisis.

This inner, personal religion is based on the American's *faith in faith*. We have seen that a primary religious affirmation of the American is his belief in religion. The American believes that religion is something very important for the community; he also believes that "faith," or what we may call religiosity, is a kind of "miracle drug" that can cure all the ailments of the spirit. It is not faith in *anything* that is so powerful, just faith, the "magic of believing." "It was back in those days," a prominent American churchman writes, recalling his early years, "that I formed a habit that I have never broken. I began saying in the morning two words, 'I believe.' Those two words *with nothing added* . . . give me a running start for my day, and for every day" (emphasis not in original).[13]

The cult of faith takes two forms, which we might designate as introvert and extrovert. In its introvert form faith is trusted to bring mental health and "peace of mind," to dissipate anxiety and guilt, and to translate the soul to the blessed land of "normality" and "self-acceptance." In earlier times this cult of faith was quite literally a cult of "faith healing," best expressed in what H. Richard Niebuhr has described as the "man-centered, this-worldly, lift-yourselves-by-your-own-bootstraps doctrine of New Thought and Christian Science."[14]

The cult of faith has also its extrovert form, and that is known as "positive thinking." "Positive thinking," thinking that is "affirmative" and avoids the corrosions of "negativity" and "skepticism," thinking that "has faith," is recommended as a powerful force in the world of struggle and achievement. Here again it is not so much faith in anything, certainly not the theocentric faith of the historic religions, that is supposed to confer this power—but just faith, the psychological attitude of having faith, so to speak. And here too the cult is largely the product of the inner disintegration and enfeeblement of the historic religions; the familiar words are retained, but the old meaning is voided. "Have faith," "Don't lose faith," and the like, were once injunctions to preserve one's unwavering trust in the God from Whom comes both the power to live and the "peace that passeth understanding." Gradually these phrases have come to be an appeal to maintain a "positive" attitude to life and not to lose confidence in oneself and one's activities. "To believe in yourself and in everything you do": such, at bottom, is the meaning of the contemporary cult of faith, whether it is proclaimed by devout men from distinguished pulpits or offered as the "secret of success" by self-styled psychologists who claim to have discovered the "hidden powers"

[13] Daniel A. Poling, "A Running Start for Every Day," *Parade: The Sunday Picture Magazine*, September 19, 1954.

[14] H. Richard Niebuhr, *The Social Sources of Denominationalism* (New York: Henry Holt & Co., 1929), p. 104.

of man. What is important is faith, faith in faith. Even where the classical symbols and formulas are still retained, that is very often what is meant and what is understood.

But side by side with America's "common faith" is the pervasiveness of religious self-identification along the tripartite scheme of Protestant, Catholic, Jew. From the "land of immigrants," America has become the "triple melting pot," restructured in three great communities with religious labels, defining three great "communions" or "faiths." This transformation has been greatly furthered by what may be called the dialectic of "third generation interest": the third generation, coming into its own with the cessation of mass immigration, tries to recover its "heritage," so as to give itself some sort of "name," or context of self-identification and social location, in the larger society. "What the son wishes to forget"—so runs "Hansen's Law"—[15] "the grandson wishes to remember." But what he can "remember" is obviously not his grandfather's foreign language, or even his grandfather's foreign culture; it is rather his grandfather's religion—America does not demand of him the abandonment of the ancestral religion as it does of the ancestral language and culture. This religion he now "remembers" in a form suitably "Americanized," and yet in a curious way, also "retraditionalized." Within this comprehensive framework of basic sociological change operate those inner factors making for a "return to religion" which so many observers have noted in recent years—the collapse of all secular securities in the historical crisis of our time, the quest for a recovery of meaning in life, the new search for inwardness and personal authenticity amid the collectivistic heteronomies of the present-day world.

Self-identification in religious terms, almost universal in the America of today, obviously makes for religious belonging in a more directly institutional way. It engenders a sense of adherence to a church or denomination and

[15] Marcus L. Hansen, *The Problem of the Third Generation Immigrant* (Augustana Historical Society, Rock Island, Ill., 1938), p. 9.

impels one to institutional affiliation. These tendencies are
reinforced by the pressures of other-directed adjustment
to peer-group behavior, which today increasingly requires
religious identification and association with some church.
Thus a pattern of religious conformism develops, most pronounced, perhaps, among the younger, "modern-minded"
inhabitants of Suburbia, but rapidly spreading to all sections of the American people.

Within the common framework, then, of the American
Religion, there is a persistent tension and conflict, reflecting the corporate anxieties and minority-group defensiveness of each of the three religious communities. But
this is not yet the ultimate ambiguity of the present religious situation in America, not the ultimate religious
conflict.

VI

The ultimate ambiguity lies in the fact that the religiousness characteristic of America today is very often a
religiousness without religion, a religiousness with almost
any kind of content or none, a way of sociability or "belonging" rather than a way of reorienting life to God. It is
thus frequently a religiousness without serious commitment, without real inner conviction, without genuine existential decision. What should reach down to the core of
existence, shattering and renewing, merely skims the surface of life, and yet succeeds in generating the sincere feeling of being religious. Religion thus becomes a kind of protection the self throws up against the radical demand of
faith.

Where the other-directed adjustment of peer-group
conformity operates, the discrepancy becomes even more
serious. The other-directed man or woman is eminently
religious in the sense of being religiously identified and
affiliated, since being religious and joining a church or
synagogue is, under contemporary American conditions,
a fundamental way of "adjusting" or "belonging." But
what can the other-directed man or woman make of the

prophets and the prophetic faith of the Bible, in which the religion of the church he joins is at least officially grounded? The very notion of being "singled out," of standing "over against" the world, is deeply repugnant to one for whom well-being means conformity and adjustment. Religion is valued as conferring a sense of sociability and "belonging," a sense of being really and truly *of* the world and society; how can the other-directed man then help but feel acutely uncomfortable with a kind of religion—for that is what biblical faith is—which is a declaration of permanent resistance to the heteronomous claims of society, community, culture, and cult? The other-directed man generally protects himself against this profoundly disturbing aspect of biblical faith by refusing to understand it; indeed, insofar as he is other-directed, he really cannot understand it. The religion he avows is still formally the Christian or Jewish faith rooted in the prophetic tradition; it is, however, so transformed as it passes through the prism of the other-directed mind that it emerges as something quite different, in many ways, its opposite. The other-directed man, no matter how religious, simply cannot understand an Elijah or an Amos, a Jesus or an Isaiah; nor can he conceivably feel any warmth of admiration for these "zealots of the Lord." Zeal, nonconformity, uncompromising witness are so "unsociable," so terribly "unadjusted"! The very purpose of the other-directed man's built-in radar apparatus is to protect him against such perils; it protects him so well that it makes the prophetic faith of the Bible almost unintelligible to him. The Christianity or Judaism he understands—and which he finds, or convinces himself that he finds, in church or synagogue—is something very different; it is an other-directed gospel of adjustment, sociability, and comfort, designed to give one a sense of "belonging," of being at home in the society and the universe. It is thus not too much of a paradox to assert that many of the inner-directed "unbelievers" of the nineteenth century in a sense stood closer to, or at least less distant from, authentic biblical faith than do so many of the religious people of our time, whose religion comes to them as an aspect of other-directed conformism and sociability.

Equally dubious from the standpoint of Jewish-Christian faith is that aspect of the present religious situation which makes religion in America so thoroughly American. Insofar as the "Americanness" of religion in America converts the three religious communions into variant expressions of American spirituality (just as the three religious communities are understood to be three subdivisions of American society), the authentic character of Jewish-Christian faith is falsified, and the faith itself reduced to the status of an American culture-religion.

This American culture-religion is the religious aspect of Americanism, conceived either as the common ground of the three "faiths" or as a kind of super-religion embracing them. It will be recalled that President Eisenhower declared "recognition of the Supreme Being" to be "the first, the most basic expression," not of our historical religions, although undoubtedly Mr. Eisenhower would agree that they are, but of . . . *Americanism*. Americanism thus has its religious creed, evoking the appropriate religious emotions; it may, in fact, be taken as the civic religion of the American people.

But civic religion has always meant the sanctification of the society and culture of which it is the reflection, and that is one of the reasons why Jewish-Christian faith has always regarded such religion as incurably idolatrous. Civic religion is a religion which validates culture and society, without in any sense bringing them under judgment. It lends an ultimate sanction to culture and society by assuring them that they constitute an unequivocal expression of "spiritual ideals" and "religious values." Religion becomes, in effect, the cult of culture and society, in which the "right" social order and the received cultural values are divinized by being identified with the divine purpose.

In a more directly political sense, this religiosity very easily comes to serve as a spiritual reinforcement of national self-righteousness and a spiritual authentication of national self-will. Americans possess a passionate awareness of their power and of the justice of the cause in which it is employed. The temptation is therefore particularly strong to identify the American cause with the cause of God, and to convert our immense and undeniable moral superiority over Communist tyranny into pretensions to unqualified wisdom and virtue. In these circumstances, it would seem to be the office of prophetic religion to raise a word of warning against inordinate national pride and self-righteousness as bound to lead to moral confusion, political irresponsibility, and the darkening of counsel. But the contemporary religious mood is very far indeed from such prophetic transcendence. Aside from occasional pronouncements by a few theologians or theologically minded clergymen, religion in America seems to possess little capacity for rising above the relativities and ambiguities of the national consciousness and bringing to bear the judgment of God upon the nation and its ways. The identification of religion with the national purpose is almost inevitable in a situation in which religion is so frequently felt to be a way of American "belonging." In its crudest form, this identification of religion with national purpose generates a kind of national messianism which sees it as the vocation of America to bring the American Way of Life, compounded almost equally of democracy and free enterprise, to every corner of the globe; in more mitigated versions, it sees God as the champion of America, endorsing American purposes, and sustaining American might. "The God of judgment has died."[16]

The burden of this criticism of American religion from the point of view of Jewish-Christian faith is that contemporary religion is so naïvely, so innocently *man-centered*. Not God, but man—man in his individual and corporate being—is the beginning and end of the spiritual system of much of present-day American religiosity. In

[16] "It is just a short step from a god who is the Great Adjuster and/or the Friendly Neighbor to the god who fights on the side of his chosen people, supporting their racial, economic or national interests . . . The God of judgment has died" (Eckard, "The New Look in American Piety," *The Christian Century*, November 17, 1954).

this kind of religion there is no sense of transcendence, no sense of the nothingness of man and his works before a holy God; in this kind of religion the values of life, and life itself, are not submitted to Almighty God to judge, to shatter, and to reconstruct; on the contrary, life, and the values of life, are given an ultimate sanction by being identified with the divine. In this kind of religion it is not man who serves God, but God who is mobilized and made to serve man and his purposes—whether these purposes be economic prosperity, free enterprise, social reform, democracy, happiness, security, or "peace of mind." God is conceived as man's "omnipotent servant,"[17] faith as a sure-fire device to get what we want. The American is a religious man, and in many cases personally humble and conscientious. But religion as he understands it is not something that makes for humility or the uneasy conscience: it is something that reassures him about the essential rightness of everything American, his nation, his culture, and himself; something that validates his goals and his ideals instead of calling them into question; something that enhances his self-regard instead of challenging it; something that feeds his self-sufficiency instead of shattering it; something that offers him salvation on easy terms instead of demanding repentance and a "broken heart." Because it does all these things, his religion, however sincere and well-meant, is ultimately vitiated by a strong and pervasive idolatrous element.

However, within the general framework of a secularized religion embracing the great mass of American people, there are signs of deeper and more authentic stirrings of faith. Duncan Norton-Taylor, in his comments on the new religiousness of businessmen, may not be altogether wrong in noting that "particularly among the younger men, there *is* a groping for a spiritual base."[18] Norman

---

[17] The phrase is from Jules H. Masserman, "Faith and Delusion in Psychotherapy: The Ur-Defenses of Man," *The American Journal of Psychiatry*, Vol. 110, No. 5, November 1953.

[18] Duncan Norton-Taylor, "Businessmen on Their Knees," *Fortune*, October, 1953.

Thomas, though recognizing that the "return to religion," which is "one of the significant phenomena of our confused and troubled times," is a "phenomenon of many and contradictory aspects," nevertheless finds it, in part at least, "definitely characterized by an awareness of, or search after God."[19] Certainly among the younger people, particularly among the more sensitive young men and women on the campuses of this country, there are unmistakable indications of an interest in, and concern with, religion that goes far beyond the demands of mere social "belonging." These stirrings are there; they are not always easily identified as religion on the one hand, or easily distinguishable from the more conventional types of religiousness on the other—but they constitute a force whose range and power should not be too readily dismissed. Only the future can tell what these deeper stirrings of faith amount to and what consequences they hold for the American religion of tomorrow.

[19] Norman Thomas, "Religion and Civilization," *The Atlantic Monthly*, August, 1947.

RELIGIOUS RESPONSIBILITY FOR THE SOCIAL ORDER:

A SYMPOSIUM BY THREE THEOLOGIANS

Jaroslav Pelikan
Gustave Weigel
Emil L. Fackenheim

A PROTESTANT VIEW

Dr. Jaroslav Pelikan

In America one can be a Protestant without being a Christian. The absence of personal commitment, which the evangelical Protestantism of America has traditionally identified as a weakness of both Roman Catholicism and the Protestant establishments of the Old World, has come to characterize the religiosity of many Americans as well. If, for example, a Roman Catholic is running for the Presidency, the non-Christian Protestants may well identify themselves as Protestants. In practice, however, their faith is an uncommitted interest in spiritual values in general and therefore a studied non-involvement in the particularity of any religious tradition. They don't even stay away from one church in particular; they stay away from all churches in general.

Most of these Protestant but non-Christian Americans would probably put the Ten Commandments or the Sermon on the Mount into first place as the source and authority for their definition of the ethical life. Unreflective though this assignment of priorities may be in many instances, it does find historical support from the vast residue of biblical terms, concepts and sanctions in the value systems both of the man on the street and the moral philosopher. It is traditional for Americans to glory in the dependence of their American morality upon the Bible. Thomas Jefferson, after all, took it upon himself to prepare an expurgated edition of the Four Gospels, as a means of assuring, he said, that Indians and others would be able to base their morals upon the authentic teachings of Jesus. More recent presidents of both parties have continued the claim—perhaps from a mixture of conviction and expediency—that biblical precedent and precept were the inspiration for their own political morality and for that of the American nation. Jefferson's domesticated version of the New Testament is likewise proof for the claim of those Americans who are Protestant but not Christian: that biblical morality may be separated from biblical doctrine. Deeds, not creeds, is only one of the many slogans by which this American tradition has sought to express its conviction that the moral teachings of Jesus, if they can be stripped of the doctrinal accretions that began with the Apostle Paul, summarize the best that men everywhere have discovered about the good life.

Careful historical research, so it was hoped, could crack the shell of the Bible, discard the husk of dogmatic theology and keep the kernel of moral truth within. Now that several generations of such research have performed their assignment, the result of their work is the disheartening discovery that for the teachings of Jesus the moral imperative was imbedded and grounded in his expectations and predictions about the coming of the Kingdom of God. What is more, although the synoptic gospels are often contrasted with the accretions added by later generations of the Christian community, these gospels themselves have been found to be the voice of the community as it remembered and celebrated the acts of God in Jesus the Christ. The Bible is consequently not a handbook of general, spiritual values but a testimony of the faith of the community in the acts of God. The presupposition of each of the Ten Commandments is the preface to the first of them: "I am the Lord, thy God, which hath brought thee out of the Land of Egypt, out of the house of bondage." The Jesus from whose remembered sayings the Sermon on the Mount was collected was the focus of the Christian liturgy and the ground of the hope of the Christian community. For historical reasons alone, and according to the Bible itself, for more than historical reasons, biblical morality is inseparable from biblical doctrine and biblical doctrine is inseparable from the community of believers. If the faith is broken off from its context in the community, and if the morality is broken off from its context in the faith, the result is a double fracture.

Although the morality may indeed be maintained for generations after both the community and its faith are gone, the Bible by itself is not enough to renew and reform the systems of value that have been drawn from it. Albert Camus says: "The problem of our time is 'How can a man become a saint without believing in God?' "

Two contrasting conclusions may be drawn from this historical analysis. It may be argued on the one hand that the case for the inseparability of biblical doctrine from the community of believers is based upon the so-called "genetic fallacy," the argument from origins. What Jesus taught, on the basis of his expectation that the end of the world was to come, may be valid even if one does not share that expectation. If an individual is told that he has six months to live and if he suddenly embarks upon moral reform as a result, he should stick to that resolve when surgery or drugs give him an unexpected reprieve. Thus, other grounds than the "dubious" metaphysics of the Bible or of the Trinitarian dogma may give better support to those elements of biblical morality that are the working value system of the American way of life. Similarly, on the other hand, other forms of common life than Israel or the Church may provide a more satisfactory matrix for our values. Now it seems to me that some such interpretation of religion in general is the conclusion to which many Americans both inside and outside the various religious traditions usually turn, when they are challenged to explain the contradiction between their protestations of religious loyalty to biblical morality, on the one hand, and their indifference or even hostility to other biblical teachings and to the continuing tradition of the community of belief.

I think such conclusions are wrong. For I think it is necessary to point out that the heritage of values bequeathed to us by Judaism and Christianity is being spent but not replenished, because the faith upon which those values were based no longer animates many of those who profess the values. To be sure, the moral habits of centuries are not easily sloughed off. People may still live as though they believed. An individual or an entire culture may remain Protestant or Roman Catholic or Eastern Orthodox long after dogmatic faith and liturgical observance have vanished. I know Protestant pietists who still will not take a drink although they have not been in church many, many years, and the Friday abstinence is one of the last things to go in marginal and apostate Roman Catholics.

When, as now, however, the crisis of history puts a system of morality to the test, then such an individual or a culture discovers, often too late, that moral values do not come equipped with a "self-starter," but that they depend for their propulsion upon sources of power beyond themselves and beyond their own culture. In each succeeding crisis—since the Babylonian captivity of Israel —the prophets of religion have issued just that warning. The effectiveness of the warning is not necessarily proportionate to its validity. The future of moral and spiritual life in America may well depend upon which of these two conclusions shapes the thinking and the teaching of this and the next generation. Can morals be separated from the teaching of the book where they are recorded? Can the book be separated from the people of God where it arises? Neither churches nor schools nor agencies like this can finally avoid a confrontation with the question of the relation between the Book of God and the People of God.

A CATHOLIC VIEW

Father Gustave Weigel, S.J.

The Christian view as I see it preaches that secular society is a distinct reality from the church which is a *sacral* society. What happens in the secular society cannot be the responsibility of the church unless by mutual contract this phase of secular life has been committed to the church by the secular society itself. When this happens the church has undertaken a secular obligation which is to be fulfilled with the instrumentalities granted by the civil secular society. If the job is not properly done, the civil society has every right to bring a charge against the church of a breach of contract. However, I do not think that this hypothesis is real anywhere in the world in which we now live. I know of no civil society today which has given the supervision of the social order to any church. Hence I say flatly today the church has no direct responsibility for the civil order anywhere because this concern lies outside the area of the church's direct action. With this said, however, I must also affirm that the church has a *preoccupation* with the social order of the secular world. It cannot be indifferent to it.

The church cannot be blamed for secular social structure nor has it the obligation to plan, control or revise it. The secular social order belongs to the secular dimension of man and therefore it looks to a dynamism other than the church for its being and efficiency. Sacral and secular authority, however, live in one and the same world, one and the same man is both sacral and secular, simultaneously under the directives of church and secular society.

The church is not the *saeculum,* but it lives, works and thinks *in saeculo.* It is of eternity, but in that sector of eternity which is fused with time. No matter what the secular power does or does not do, the church must teach its own concept of social fellowship and must demand that in its own closed community such a vision be respected and, as far as human fragility permits, be actualized. This will be conditioned, of course, by the secular component of human life. All religions—which in this address I call the church—teach ascetical self-control, at least to the degree of effective submission to just law even when the law is purely secular. All religions believe in the virtues of equity, sobriety and honesty. All religions somehow have a vision of the universal fellowship of men. These virtues contribute immensely to a beneficent secular social order. Where these virtues thrive the secular social order is healthy and dynamic. Police power cannot produce these virtues, but the church can inculcate them better than any other agency.

The fatal enemy of any social order is individual and collective selfishness. The church, because it teaches man that he is not the Lord but under the Lord, necessarily strives to inculcate unselfishness. Unselfishness can exist in men who are not orientated to God. But such men are few. For the generality, religion alone engenders an atmosphere of unselfishness. The energy of the church is of great importance, therefore, to the well-being of the secular social order. Hence, secular powers, for their own ends, should foster the work of the church which itself is not for their end.

The church promotes virtue without primarily intending the good of secular society. It does so only because it is the will of God, the Lord of both the church and of secular society. Even if secular society were totally uninterested the church would still have the mission of preaching virtue. The church in just being the church helps secular society by way of by-product. The church, therefore, must do its own work. In doing its own work for no secular purpose it aids the secular society. That society has no right to ask the church to do more.

Church meddling in the secular order has brought grief both to the churches and to secular societies. We must not secularize the church either in the name of the church or in the name of the secular community which is precisely the temptation which faces us in America.

Under no circumstances should an unbelieving secular society for its own ends use the church which, by constitution and dedication, is above the secular society's concern. What is more, the church in her prophetic role as the spokesman of God must prophesy to the secular community. The church must stoutly condemn the world's injustices, not only in the abstract, but in the concrete, and preach to the world the true concept of man as seen in divine revelation. Such prophecy will rarely be accepted and usually the prophet will receive the prophet's reward—persecution and stoning.

We must not enlist the church, a community of believers, in a campaign to save the secular society or enhance its power. This the church cannot do. As men interested in the secular good of our secular society, we must see that all we can do is urge the church to be genuinely herself. When she is that, by way of by-product, good will adhere to the secular society in which the church is only a lodger.

The Kingdom of God to which the church is committed will come only by God's power and not by the vitiated strength of man. The Kingdom of God will come not *in saeculo* but when that saeculum is finished.

A JEWISH VIEW

Rabbi Emil L. Fackenheim

If there is a single religious affirmation which, first coming with Judaism into the world, has remained basic to Jewish belief until today, it is that the God on high loves widows and orphans below; and that He commands men, from on high, to do His will in the social order below. Elsewhere, too, men have had an awareness of the Divine, and a sense of responsibility in the social realm. It was the distinctive contribution of the Hebrew prophets to proclaim that the two cannot be rent apart; that men ought to treat each other as created in the image of a God who challenges them to this task.

II

It is in the light of this basic affirmation that I must seek to answer the question concerning religious responsibility for the social order. And I must begin by opposing all attempts to tear asunder what the prophetic affirmation joins together; that is, on the one hand, a secularism which bids religion mind its business, of which responsibility for the social order is to be no part, and, on the other hand, an otherworldly religion which, accepting this advice, disclaims all responsibility for the social order. Forms of such divorce have existed in all ages. That they may exist in one and the same person has been terribly illustrated in our own time—by those Germans who thought it possible to be Nazis and Christians at once.

I must stress that opposing divorce between the religious and the social realm is by no means equivalent to rejecting the separation between church and state, of which more below. I must stress, too, that secularist social morality has often put to shame a social morality supposedly religiously inspired; that those rejecting or suspending belief in God have often done His will toward men more perfectly than those professing belief in Him. And this fact must give us pause. Even so, one may question whether secularist morality can, for long, treat men as created in the image of a God in Whom it does not believe; whether it can forever resist the temptation to reduce man, from an end in himself, to a mere means, thus degenerating either into a merely relativistic morality, or else—and worse—into one resting on pseudo-absolutes, such as the interests of a deified class, nation or state.

The dangers of divorce between the religious and the social may seem remote to North Americans, who tend to be practical in religion and religiously inspired in their social morality; and indeed, for the worst examples of divorce we must surely look elsewhere. Still, we are by no means exempt from danger. For a religious civilization such as ours invites a secularism assuming a pseudo-religious garb; and hence religion, meant to be openness to the divine imperative, may become a device for avoiding it. Thus, for example, those who begin by responding to the divine imperative, with a dedication to freedom and democracy, may end up deifying their dedication; and to the extent to which they in fact do so their actual dedication—as well as what it is dedicated to—is perverted. Of this danger, there are ominous indications in our time.

III

So much for the divorce between the religious and the social, which the prophetic imperative bids us oppose. What of their relation, which that imperative bids us affirm? This question, unlike the former, is fraught with great difficulty. And its essential cause is that, while the prophetic imperative is divine, the social world in which it is to find realization is human; and the human world has characteristics which render complex, not only any attempt to *realize* the prophetic imperative, but even any attempt—such as the present—merely to *state* it, in terms concrete enough to be applicable. Three characteristics must here be noted.

(1) All social organization involves power. But power is amoral before it can be made moral, and presumably it always retains aspects of amorality or even immorality. This fact confronts those who would heed the prophetic imperative with a dilemma. They may either forswear all use of power, in order to remain true to the prophetic imperative. But then they condemn their own efforts to ineffectiveness, at least beyond the most private relations and in the social order as a whole; and thus they contribute either to total anarchy or else—more likely—to an amoral order based on naked power. Yet most forms of social order are better than anarchy, and a partly moralized order better than one not moralized at all. Alternatively, they may seek power, for the sake of the prophetic imperative which demands realization. But then they must recognize that they become compromised in

its use; and their religious motivation is no protection against such compromise. Indeed, experience shows that power wielded in the name of God is subject to special perversions.

This is why those who are organized by commitment to the prophetic imperative cannot, on the one hand, escape their responsibility of moralizing power, while on the other hand they must resist all temptations to make a bid for direct power, confining themselves to indirect methods of pressure-by-exhortation. Here lies perhaps the deepest justification for the American principle of the separation of state and church.

(2) What must be the content of such exhortation? May religion advocate specific measures in the name of God, leaving to the state and society the task of their enactment? Here I come upon a second complexity of the human condition, which makes such a neat arrangement impossible. This is that concrete moral ends are, in the actual human situation, in conflict both with other ends and with the means required to enact them. I cannot think of a single moral and religious end, concrete enough to be directly applicable, and yet valid without exception. Thus believing all human life to be sacred I believe all wars to be evil; and yet I must admit that some wars had justly to be fought. But the concept of "just war" does not supply me with universally applicable criteria. Again, though believing in the Biblical injunction to be fruitful and multiply I cannot deduce from this belief the universal wrongness of artificial birth control. For I must measure the Biblical injunction against the dangers of overpopulation and mass-starvation. In short, I find myself unable to subscribe to what has been called the natural law, supplying us with a knowledge of right and wrong sufficiently concrete to be directly applicable, and yet valid regardless of time and circumstances.

(3) Must religion, then, confine itself to the affirmation of abstract principles, leaving to other forces not merely the task of enactment but also that of specific application? Is religion confined to affirming in general the sacredness of life and liberty, and the evil of exploitation, but

barred from taking a specific stand as to when life may be taken and liberty curtailed; and as to what constitutes a just minimum wage? Here we are come upon this further characteristic of the human condition, that the moral and religious conscience of a society is manifest, not in an abstract affirmation of liberty or condemnation of exploitation, but in what it protests against, as constituting a case of curtailed liberty, or a case of exploitation. Relevancy lies in the particular. As for the general, this is apt to be invoked not only by the indifferent but even by the enemy; peace has been invoked by the mongers of war, freedom and democracy, by their worst foes. This tendency to hypocrisy is evident throughout human history. But, as George Orwell has shown with such depressing persuasiveness, not until the twentieth century have men made it into a system.

Another neat arrangement of the respective responsibilities of religion and society for the social order has thus collapsed. A religion which confines itself to general principles condemns itself to ineffectiveness and innocuousness. The Hebrew prophets, in contrast, were neither innocuous nor ineffective. And this was because they asserted the will of God, not in terms of abstract general principles, but in and for the here and now.

IV

In the light of these reflections, how, then, can I link, positively and concretely, prophetic religion to its responsibilities for the social order? The link is found, I think, not in rules or principles but in a believing attitude.

This believing attitude must, first, stubbornly insist that the will of God is to be done in the social world of man, and that we are responsible for our share in it. It must resist the temptation, born of the frustrations of all ages and especially of our own, of escaping into dualism, whether into a divine world above, unconcerned with man, or into a human world below, unconcerned with God and hence not really human.

This believing attitude must, first, stubbornly insist that the will of God exists, not in general, or for some other place and time, but here and now. There is no situation which is morally and religiously neutral. There is no power-struggle, however necessarily Machiavellian, which is not at the same time a situation in which the prophetic imperative speaks to us. And even the thunder of nuclear tests must not be allowed to drown its voice.

Thirdly, the prophetic imperative, being divine, must be taken with radical seriousness, not given mere half-hearted and niggardly concessions. It is one thing to be forced to compromise in the struggle against war, oppression, discrimination and poverty, and to accept such compromises temporarily and with an aching heart. It is another thing entirely to mistake what are at best incomplete achievements finally and self-righteously, as if they were perfect. This believing attitude can never forget that so long as the divine image is violated even in one single human being, the Kingdom of God on earth is incomplete.

Fourthly, this believing attitude knows that while the prophetic imperative is divine even our best efforts to respond to it are only human. And this is true not only of our organized forms of acting but also of our organized forms of belief, doctrine and preaching. Society and religion, even at their best, are under the judgment of God.

Finally and most importantly, this believing attitude knows that while we have our responsible share in the doing of God's will in the social world of man, the fate of that world is not in our hands alone. Throughout the ages, those committed to the prophetic imperative have always been threatened by despair, when faced with the discrepancy between what ought to be and what is. This danger assumes unheard-of proportions in a world confronted with possibilities of total destruction. Today, more than ever, one can heed the prophetic imperative with any kind of confidence only if one heeds it with an ultimate confidence; with the confidence in a God who, while bidding us to work in His world, is also its absolute Sovereign.

RELIGIOUS LIBERTY FROM THE VIEWPOINT OF A SECULAR HUMANIST

Sidney Hook

My first proposition is that an open, democratic society does not rest on any religious or metaphysical presuppositions, and that its justification is to be found in its empirical consequences as contrasted with the consequences of living in non-democratic societies. Belief in the validity of democratic society therefore is compatible with many different religious and metaphysical presuppositions, but logically it does not rest upon any. It is sometimes said that democracy rests upon the belief in "the brotherhood of man under the fatherhood of God." But such a belief is not a *necessary* logical condition for democracy, since democracy is a system which depends upon men being equal, in certain respects, before the Law independently of whether they are regarded as equal in the sight of the Lord. The brotherhood of man, whether taken as a theological or biological fact, does not of itself tell us how to act towards one another—whether like the first pair of brothers, Cain and Abel, or like Jonathan and David, who were not brothers. Neither is this belief a *sufficient* condition for democracy. Most religions have sanctified undemocratic societies in the past. Franco's Spain is not a democratic society nor is Salazar's Portugal, although both profess belief in the Judaic-Christian tradition.

If this is true, then it is impermissible for a democratic society to make the acceptance of any religious or metaphysical presupposition a condition of genuine citizenship within it or of the effective exercise of the duties of citizenship. Individuals of all religions or no religion enjoy the same status as citizens providing they accept the rules of the democratic game. No one should be penalized for his religious belief; no one should be required to subscribe to any religious ideology as a condition precedent for exercising his rights of citizenship. *This makes religion a private matter with no responsibility on the part of the state to support it in any way.* For if the state supports one religion, it thereby compels those who subscribe to other religions to shoulder both the expense and responsibility of such support, neither of which can be justified by any rational defense of democracy. And if the state supports all religions, it compels those who subscribe to no religion, who have the same rights as citizens as their neighbors, to support what they do not believe in and in what is not required for the proper functioning of the democratic process.

This is the logic or ideal of commitment to an open society, whatever the historical facts in the past may have been. Insofar as the state moves towards neutrality in matters of religious belief and practice, it moves towards greater democracy. For it thereby recognizes the autonomy of moral and political experience with respect to religion. To fail to distinguish between the historical and ideal moments in this process is to invite the confusions which mark Supreme Court opinions on the meaning of the First Amendment: i.e., certain conclusions which are in consonance with the rationale of the democratic society are read back into the historical language of the Constitution, despite the obvious fact that in the early years of the imperfect, developing democracy of the United States, these words were understood in the light of contemporary religious practices.

We may test this analysis by examining Mr. Justice Douglas' well-known observation in Zorach *v.* Clauson (1952): "We are a religious people whose institutions presuppose a Supreme Being." That we are a religious people is a true historical statement, from which nothing follows to our purpose, for it is equally compatible both with the view that religion is and should be a private matter and with the contrary view that religion is and

should be a matter of public concern. The statement
that our institutions presuppose the existence of a Supreme
Being is a much more momentous assertion. It obviously
is not an historical statement but an analytical one. It
asserts that the validity of the institutions which constitute the American way of life depends upon the existence
of a Supreme Being as a necessary condition—from which
it follows that if the existence of a Supreme Being were
denied, belief in the validity of our political institutions
would not be warranted.

If it could be established that the validity of the democratic process rests upon belief in a Supreme Being, then
those who believe that the democratic state should publicly encourage and support religious belief and practice would have gone a long way toward establishing
their position. Indeed, to believe in democratic institutions on this basis, and not to encourage respect for its
foundations, would be evidence of flagrant inconsistency.
Conversely, if Justice Douglas' statement were true it
would follow that anyone who is critical of belief in a
Supreme Being or who is irreligious, is undermining, to
the extent that ideas influence action, the very foundations of democracy.

It is extremely puzzling to understand how Justice
Douglas can square his belief in this proposition and his
judicial opinions, but this is a peripheral question. I am
not interested in plumbing Justice Douglas' mind, but in
testing the validity of his position. The central question
is: is his statement true? What specific American institution rests upon the existence of a Supreme Being or
belief in him? Is it our method of nomination and elections, our judicial system, our free enterprise system to
the extent it is free, our practices under the Bill of Rights,
our welfare legislation? I think it is demonstrable that
there is no inherent connection between belief or disbelief in the existence of a Supreme Being and any one
of those institutions. Belief in God has indeed been conjoined with belief in these institutions, but it has also been
conjoined with quite different institutions without logical
or theological consistency. Some religious persons have

even argued that to seek divine sanction for institutional arrangements which reflect the shifting prudential necessities of human beings in their quest for public order and personal freedom borders on the blasphemous. At any rate, no religion based on a vision of, or belief in, an order of experience transcending nature and history, can intelligibly show how the element of the transcendent can function as a *univocal* guide to the choices men face in the temporal and contingent world. Every such derivation is question-begging or circular. "God" has been enrolled under all banners, including those arrayed against each other.

The historical evidence reinforces this conclusion. The history of religious struggle and conflicts has not been *primarily* an attempt to increase the sphere of political and personal freedom, but rather to exercise domination with respect to religious dogma or practice or to win independence of such domination. There is overwhelming evidence to support Figgis' trenchant observation: "Political liberty is the residuary legatee of ecclesiastical animosities." Religious tolerance has developed more as a consequence of the impotence of religions to impose their dogmas on each other than as a consequence of spiritual humility in the quest for understanding first and last things.

II

Although there are no logical lines of connection between a belief in transcendent reality and specific social and political institutions, a democracy must countenance the largest possible latitude towards expressions of religious belief. This is part of its policy of encouraging the existence and activity of voluntary associations among its citizens free to criticize each other as well as the central political authority whose virtue and wisdom should always be open to question even when its sovereignty is acknowledged. There need be therefore no limits whatsoever placed on freedom of religious thought. Very few religions in principle grant this right to other religions save on prudential grounds. To the extent that any religion makes a claim to possession of the absolute truth concerning man's natural or supernatural end, and to be the sole and unique authority in interpreting that end, it tends to regard the propagation of other religious doctrines as a threat to human salvation. It is, of course, quite natural that belief in religious truth should entail opposition to religious error. I find it difficult to conceive of a religion which makes belief in Something without further specification a sufficient description of religious commitment or which emphasizes faith in Faith without delimiting the objects of faith. The very sincerity with which a religious truth is believed is an index of implied opposition to religious error. Although it is easy to make a distinction abstractly between the heretic and his heresy, the disbeliever and his disbelief, in practice, where the avowal of any religious truth becomes a responsibility of the public or civil order, there is a constant danger that the rights of citizens who subscribe to different religious "truths" or to no religious truths at all may be abridged. This is all the more reason why the democratic open society must observe a strict neutrality towards all religious creeds independently of the changes in the relative political strength of members of different religions. It does not deny the right of members of *any* religious group to speak their minds about political issues. It defends that right against any who would prevent its expression. It condemns only the attempt to mobilize religious sentiment for political action of a kind which results either in making the *religious* conscience of one group legally binding on the behavior of all groups or, by linking matters of public policy that should be open to discussion to religious dogmas that are not likely to receive critical discussion, encourages a fanaticism which makes the spirit of tolerance and reasonable compromise impossible.

This view that the public or civil order must not be invaded by any religious group for purposes of partisan advantage—and any proposal or practice that some religious or non-religious group regards as an interference with the integrity of its own faith must be carefully examined for evidence of partisanship—has sometimes been interpreted as a disguised enmity toward all religion, to a sectarian secularism which is really not neutral but hostile to religion. There is no justification for the charge. The influence of religion in American society has grown very markedly despite the fact that certain religious observances in the public order have been curtailed. The change in the temper of the American people may be gauged from the fact that about eighty years ago it was possible for a famous freethinker like Robert Ingersoll to place the name of James G. Blaine in nomination at the presidential convention of the Republican Party. Today this would hardly be likely. The very growth in the intensity of religious feeling, thought and writing and the rise in denominational affiliation bespeak not a retreat before an irreligious secular offensive, but an increase of religious pressures on the public order. It is this awareness among the religious and non-religious alike that differences in religious belief, if they obtrude into the public order as they unfortunately have, may become focal points of religious conflict, which has led to the assertion of the principle of religious neutrality on the part of the democratic state. Whether it represents a reassertion of a principle accepted during the founding years of the republic, I leave to those historians better informed than I to say. Whether it represents a constitutional innovation or a plain reading of a plain text depends upon who reads the Constitution. But that it expresses the wisdom of a democratic polity in a community of plural religious faiths, I have no doubt.

III

I approach now some of the more difficult problems connected with my theme. We speak of religious freedom, and insofar as religious *thought* is concerned, one may innocently speak of such freedom without limits. But religion, whatever else it may be, is associated with ritual and practice. Wherever there exist practices or actions that involve others, we cannot recognize absolutes. This means that freedom of religious practice must be subject to some control as it always has been in the past. We do not today in this country permit the practice of any religion which involves human sacrifice, plural marriage, and the use of dangerous animals like rattlesnakes in worship. There is no point in being mealy-mouthed about it. When we say that each individual may worship God according to his conscience, we always presuppose that such worship falls within the permissible limits of morality. Most of the religions of the West are agreed in their basic moral values. This has not always been so and may not always be so in the future. And there is a large variety of religious practices, outside of the Western tradition, which we would condemn, ranging from sacred prostitution to suttee.

The primacy of morality to religion is the most fundamental reason for preserving the independence and neutrality of the state. For religious dogmas, or rather the practices allegedly derived from them, often run counter to the principles of an enlightened morality. I am not saying that the sole function of the state is to impose a code of minimum morality on the community and certainly not that it is the sole source or repository of morality. Not all law is concerned with morals, and some laws may be immoral. Nor am I denying that religious groups may reinforce the moral principles of a community or even with prophetic zeal call community and state practices to account. What I am maintaining is the autonomy of moral judgment in relation to any distinctive religious belief, and the responsibility of the community, especially the democratic community, to resolve moral conflicts on the basis of the relevant moral issues which rise afresh in each generation.

The retort is sometimes made that moral values are logically dependent upon transcendent religious beliefs and that the validity of the first presupposes the validity of the second. But analysis shows that it is impossible to derive moral predicates from any statement of existence, transcendent or natural, unless these moral predicates have been surreptitiously introduced into the existential predicates. Men do not derive their morality from their belief in the existence of God; on the contrary, men conceive of God in their own moral image. A moral insight may be expressed in the language of religious dogma, but it is always possible to disentangle the kernel of moral wisdom from the theological husk. Sometimes this is granted and the contention advanced that although the meaning and validity of ethical statements are logically independent of any religious or metaphysical statement, in *fact* or in *practice*, moral behavior rests upon belief in religious dogma. For example, Dr. Robert Hutchins maintains that "whereas it may be theoretically possible for a man to be good without being religious, it is not practically possible for a man to be good without being religious." I believe everyone knows some good men who are not religious, and is aware that there is no concomitant variation between a person's religious piety and his goodness, and not only because of differences in religious morality. If individual virtue is primarily a matter of habit, then we must look to the habits of action acquired in early youth to explain goodness. These habits may be, and sometimes obviously are, independent of the religious dogmas which accompany them.

Any statement about the influence of religious belief on moral practice, once it is admitted that there is no necessary connection between them, is a statement of psychology or social psychology and subject to empirical tests. One can predict the moral behavior of individuals more reliably on the basis of their early habits than on the basis of any other factor. There are other factors of which we must take note, especially when children have reached the age of reason. One can teach kindness and truthfulness to the young on the basis of *plural* justifications, the most persuasive of which are their fruits in experience.

It is important to recognize the supremacy, or rather the logical priority, of the ethical issue where religious standpoints seem to conflict on a specific question because, unless the question is treated as a moral one which invites rational inquiry, what we have is a confrontation of religious absolutes, all appealing to some transcendental source, without being able to indicate an objective method by which differences may be resolved. The moral issue is then befogged by considerations which belong to an entirely different order. The democratic open society must be neutral to all religious overbeliefs, but no matter how secular it conceives itself to be, it cannot be neutral to moral issues. It seeks to draw these issues into the area of public discussion in the hope that a reasonable consensus may be achieved. So long as the questions of planned parenthood or birth control or therapeutic abortion are approached from the standpoint of theological doctrine, their resolution is impossible in a pluralistic society of competing theological faiths. Where they are approached as ethical questions, the prospects of agreement are much better. If agreement is won on the ethical issue then, as the history of theological doctrine shows, sometimes changes are made in the meaning and range of applicability of theological dogmas which make certain practices formerly acceptable presently unacceptable, and vice versa.

This enables us to distinguish between the freedom to propagate one's religious faith, and the freedom to use the political processes of a democratic society as a convenient strategy to further this faith. Within the limits of the morally permissible, every religious faith is a law unto itself, since membership in it is voluntary, and the burdens it imposes on its members having been freely accepted, may be freely laid aside without suffering secular sanctions. It can excommunicate recalcitrant individuals from its church but it cannot excommunicate them from the political community. If a religious group believes that marriage is a sacrament which should never be dissolved by divorce, or that certain foods are tabooed because of a divine command, it may live within the discipline of its faith. But if it seeks to impose its conception of marriage or its dietary predilections upon the rest of the community, it is violating the ethos of the open society, and mocks its profession of belief in religious freedom.

The grounds on which a position is taken are of the first importance here. Any individual may oppose divorce on moral and social grounds; any individual may seek to extend the pure food laws to certain articles of diet on grounds of public health and welfare. When he does this, he acts as a citizen with a citizen's right to be wrong, and not as a member of a disciplined religious group voting to make his particular religious dogma binding upon others. He presumably is open to argument and evidence of an empirical kind. It is one thing to advocate prohibition and a ban against national lotteries on the ground that such legislation furthers the public welfare. Individuals of all religious faiths or none may subscribe to the proposal. But it is something else again to propose that gambling and the consumption of liquor should be forbidden by law because they are *sinful* according to some religious dogmas. A democratic community may recognize—indeed, it must recognize—what is morally evil, but it cannot recognize the category of sin, legislate against it and punish those for whom the proscribed action is not sinful. One man's sin may be another man's duty and a third man's bliss. Even if a religious group commands a majority in a democratic community, it has no justification, according to the spirit of democratic policy, to legislate against sin. Such action is an invitation to religious civil war. Usually when there is sufficient evidence that something is evil or socially undesirable to a point where legal action seems indicated, it is unnecessary to introduce theological dogma to support proposals to cope with it. It is only when persuasive moral argument is lacking, or when, as in the case of therapeutic abortion and some other measures of birth control, the moral argument for the practice is overwhelmingly cogent, that recourse is made to theological dogma. But in a community of plural and incompatible religious faiths, at any point where a theological dogma is introduced to control public policy, it is a dagger thrust at the very heart of the political democratic process.

I should like to conclude by re-emphasizing two points which are often overlooked. The first involves a misconception about the nature of secularism previously mentioned. There seems to be a recurrent belief that a consistent secularism must itself develop into a religious doctrine which makes an idol of the state. Worship of the state—of any state, it is alleged—is a form of totalitarianism, which if not as extreme as fascism or communism, belongs to the same genus. This criticism is directed especially against those secularists who misguidedly speak of "the religion of democracy."

If we understand by democracy a political system which is based on a free market in ideas and unwavering allegiance to the institutions that make it possible, then I believe it can be shown that such criticism is unjust. The democratic state is not an object, or, in the first instance, a power, but a set of processes which enable us to derive a common public policy from conflicting public opinions. Although it has its rites and symbols, it does not command the total or even the supreme allegiance of anyone. Within the limits of public morality, it permits individuals to worship at any private altar. Within the limits of public order and the necessities of public welfare, limits which cannot be repudiated except by anarchists, it acknowledges the legitimacy of plural authorities. It therefore has no party line in science or chess, art or music, philosophy or theology or any other theoretical discipline. Those who see in secularism a mask of latter-day Jacobinism or Bolshevism are terrorizing themselves by fancies born of historical ignorance and defective logic. It is simply false to say of any democratic secularists that they make "all authority which does not reside in the state an opponent of the well-being of the body politic." The family, the church, the school, the trade union, the professional association are all recognized as sources of authority in a democratic community. The area of their competence is freely acknowledged. It is only when the authority of a private association seeks to usurp public authority and exploit the agencies of the state to hold the allegiance of its adult members, or to impose that allegiance on others, that the democratic state intervenes. The persecution of religion by communist states is a consequence, not of their secularism, but of their political and cultural dictatorship.

The enlightened secularist regards public or political life as far from being the only or most important dimension of life. It constitutes only a small part of what Santayana calls "natural society," and its greatest virtue is to provide the conditions for "free society" and "ideal society," those pastures of the spirit in which in voluntary companionship men cultivate their interests in art, science, and religion. When a secularist says that religion is a private matter, we must remember that for him, as for any other reflective person, the private is a vast realm which the public life of a democracy defends against arbitrary incursion. The greater the interdependence among us, enforced by the consequences of growth in technology and population, the more precious does the private and personal become. No democratic secularist or humanist seeks, for example, to give the state a monopoly of the processes of education. At most the state can require that certain minimum standards of literacy, of skills and information be upheld. Any other education may be given by any private agency, including the church. But no private agency has a claim upon the state to underwrite its program of instruction.

My second concluding point is directed to those who have a passionate concern for religious truth, who are convinced that they possess it, and who accept the Augustinian dictum that where the truth is known men have not the right to err. I have a profound respect for those who, like myself, are concerned with religious truth. Although I have suffered a lifelong frustration in not being able to find any religious truth, my mind is not closed to its possibility. Now whatever the meaning of the expression "religious truth" is, its connotation must embrace that of the term "truth." This is an important truism. In all other contexts in which we declare something to be true our warrant is derived either from logic or from evidence or experience. Revelation presumably is a report of experience. Whether the grounds of the assertion of truth are logical or experiential, they must be apparent to me. If they are apparent to me, if I am persuaded that I know the truth, then it is completely pointless to say that I have no right to err. But if the grounds are not apparent to me but to someone else, then it is not merely pointless for someone else to say I have no right to err, but false, monstrously false. For *my* mind cannot be coerced into belief on the strength of someone else's thinking or experiencing. To deny me the right to err is therefore to deny me the right to believe. It is to deny me the right to be a person. To use the state directly or indirectly to impose sanctions on me for my erring belief or lack of belief is not to act out of desire to further the truth—since no one can be persuaded of truth in this manner—but to act from power. It is to impose arbitrarily personal or organizational power where the proper means of persuasion have failed. In a community where several religious faiths believe they have the truth, the claim that there is no right to err with respect to it opens the door to the furies of religious fanaticism.

That is why those who believe in religious truth, and are interested in establishing agreement on the basis of reason and evidence, would do well to take as their model the ethics and logic of scientific inquiry. Despite the fact, nay, *because* of the fact, that the scientific community recognizes that every inquirer has the right to err, that every statement is open to doubt, that nothing is asserted to be certain, that progress is made by the refutation of hypotheses—it achieves a far greater measure of uncoerced agreement about the nature of things than is the case in those fields in which the loudest and most frequent claims to certain or absolute knowledge are heard.

Religious *freedom* in an open society has the best prospects of flourishing to the extent that it expresses itself as freedom of religious *inquiry*. Genuine inquiry—that is, inquiry not tethered to a predetermined conclusion—puts something in risk, in a quest for a truth which can never be absolute. The "fallibilism" of Charles Peirce and John Dewey expresses the faith of the American open society that all men can live peacefully together in their search for satisfying truths.

FREEDOM AND SEPARATION: AMERICA'S CONTRIBUTION TO CIVILIZATION

Leo Pfeffer

America has made many contributions to civilization, but none equals, and certainly none exceeds, the contribution epitomized in the first sixteen words of the Bill of Rights: "Congress shall make no law respecting an establishment of religion or prohibiting the free exercise thereof."

Indeed, David Dudley Field, one of America's great jurists, went considerably further when, in the latter half of the nineteenth century he stated:

> The greatest achievement ever made in the cause of human progress is the total and final separation of church and state. If we had nothing else to boast of, we could lay claim with justice that first among the nations we of this country made it an article of organic law that the relations between man and his Maker were a private concern, into which other men have no right to intrude. To measure the stride thus made for the emancipation of the race, we have only to look back over the centuries that have gone before us, and recall the dreadful persecutions in the name of religion that have filled the world.

Field's estimation may be too extreme. Nevertheless, it seems to me that of all the freedoms that Americans enjoy, of all the liberties which are part of our heritage, none exceeds religious freedom in importance.

First, I suggest that, at least in the American system, religious freedom is the progenitor of practically all other

freedoms. The Bill of Rights—that is, the first ten amendments to the Constitution—safeguards a variety of freedoms
and liberties. The First Amendment, after prohibiting an
establishment of religion or interference with its free exercise, declares that Congress shall likewise make no law
"abridging the freedom of speech, or of the press, or of
the right of the people peaceably to assemble and to
petition for a just redress of grievances." Other liberties
secured in the following amendments include the right
to a fair trial, the right of one charged with a crime not to
be compelled to incriminate himself, the right to counsel,
the right to be informed of the nature of the offense with
which one is charged, the right not to be placed in double
jeopardy or be tried more than once for the same offense,
and the right not to be subjected to cruel and unusual
punishments. An examination of Anglo-American history
will reveal, I believe, that all these rights and liberties
came about as a direct and, in fact, inevitable consequence
of the successful struggle of Englishmen and Americans
for religious freedom.

Consider freedom of speech. Today it is generally
thought of in terms of political speech: the right of the
radical, the malcontent, the street-corner agitator to attack
the government and condemn its policies, even perhaps to
advocate revolutionary overthrow of the government. Historically, however, freedom of political speech came late
on the scene; it came after freedom of religious speech
had been won. The struggle for freedom of speech in
England, from which we inherited our tradition, was
initially a struggle for freedom to speak religiously, for
freedom to speak in a manner deemed heretical by the
established church. As late as 1774, James Madison found
it necessary to write to a friend that:

> That diabolical, hell-conceived principle of persecu
> tion rages among some. . . . This vexes me the worst
> of anything whatever. There are at this time in the
> adjacent county not less than five or six well-meaning
> men in close jail for publishing their religious senti
> ments, which in the main are very orthodox. I have

neither patience to hear, talk, or think of anything relative to this matter; for I have squabbled and scolded, abused and ridiculed, so long about it to little purpose, that I am without common patience. So I must beg you to pity me, and pray for liberty of conscience to all.

By the time the Constitution was written in 1787 and the Bill of Rights added in 1791, the war for freedom of religious speech had been won. The persecution and martyrdom suffered by those who would not forego the demands of their conscience had borne fruit. The Cromwellian revolution, the Restoration, the Toleration Act of 1689, the Virginia Declaration of Rights, and Jefferson's monumental Statute Establishing Religious Freedom combined to establish as a self-evident truth that freedom of religious speech was an inalienable, natural right of all men.

If freedom of religious speech was a natural right of man, it followed logically and inevitably that so too was freedom of non-religious speech. If one could speak freely of the sacred, he certainly could speak freely of the secular. If silence on matters of eternal truths and values could not lawfully be imposed by government, logic required that it could not be imposed in respect to the less important domain of temporal affairs. When the First Amendment came to be written, and it had already been established that Americans and Englishmen had a natural right to speak freely of religious matters, it followed inevitably that they had a right to speak freely of other matters. Thus freedom of speech was written into the Bill of Rights.

What is true of freedom of speech is equally true of freedom of the press. This too is today generally conceived of in terms of political or possibly aesthetic expression. But its origin is to be found in the struggle for freedom of the religious press. As is well known, for a long time it was an offense punishable even by burning at the stake to print the Bible in the common tongue so that it could be read by others than the priests. Printing religious tracts which strayed even slightly from the orthodox was likewise a punishable offense. It was the great glory of the Puritan revolution that it established in most of the English domains the right freely to print religious books, tracts, and pamphlets. When that right was established, it followed that Englishmen and Americans had the equivalent right to print non-religious, political, aesthetic, and scientific books, tracts, and pamphlets. That, too, was written into the Constitution as part of the Bill of Rights.

The same is true in respect to freedom of assembly. We generally consider this to be a political right—the right to hold a mass meeting to demand the end of nuclear bomb testing or recognition of Red China. However, its origin in Anglo-American tradition was religious assembly, the right to assemble to worship together in a manner not permitted by the established church. When the right of religious assembly was won, inevitably the right of political assembly followed.

Even those rights which seem far removed from religion —the right not to incriminate oneself, to confront one's accusers, not to be subjected to double jeopardy or cruel and unusual punishments—found their way into our Bill of Rights as a consequence of the struggle for religious liberty. These rights came out of the religious or heresy trials of the Star Chamber in the sixteenth and seventeenth centuries. "Freedom" John Lilburne, a Puritan leveler, religious dissenter, and heretic, was one of the heroes of the struggle for fair trial. In his frequent encounters with the Star Chamber he continually asserted his rights as an Englishman not to be compelled to incriminate himself, to have counsel to assist him in his defense, and to be informed of the nature of the offense with which he was charged. He and others asserted these rights in heresy trials, and one by one they came to be accepted as natural rights of Englishmen. And so they too found their way into our Constitution and Bill of Rights.

Thus religious freedom is the progenitor of practically all our freedoms and in that respect is the most important of them. When the state was ready to grant religious freedom to its citizens, it was soon ready to grant them other freedoms. Conversely, if a state is prepared to deprive its citizens of their rights in matters of conscience, it is inevitable that it will soon deprive them of all other rights.

The second item of evidence in support of my suggestion that religious freedom is the most important of all our freedoms is also to be found in our history. I do not suppose that any statistics have or indeed could practicably be made on this, yet I believe that if at the time our Constitution was written a statistical table could have been made of the causes for which throughout history men have shed the blood of other men, on the top of the list would be the cause of religion. Up to the time of our Constitution, it is probable that more blood had been shed for what man claimed to be the greater glory of God than for any other cause in history.

We still shed blood. We still have wars. Men still take arms against each other and engage in wholesale slaughter of human beings. We have many reasons for engaging in war—political, economic, nationalistic reasons. But we no longer pretend that we do so because God wishes us to. We no longer commit that terrible sacrilege of saying "Thy will be done" when we drop an atomic bomb on a city.

Religious wars are happily a matter of history. No longer do men resort to arms to coerce other men to worship God as the sword-bearers deem to be the only true method of worship. I suggest to you that a major cause of this turn of events was the launching of the American experiment of religious freedom and the separation of church and state. Today there is hardly a nation in the world having a written constitution which does not contain some recognition of freedom of worship. And it is this universal emulation of the American experiment which has brought to an end the religious wars and persecutions that have plagued Europe for well nigh two thousand years.

What is this American experiment that is epitomized in the first sixteen words of the Bill of Rights? The opening words of the First Amendment speak of establishment of religion and prohibition of its free exercise. The ban on establishment of religion has become popularized in Jefferson's metaphor of a wall of separation between church and state. The term separation of church and state has been criticized on the one hand by some law school professors and on the other by certain Roman Catholic spokesmen. The former point out that the term is not to be found in the Constitution; the latter that it is vague, misleading, and basically inconsistent with America's friendship to religion.

I do not find any need to defend the phrase "separation of church and state" as an exercise in English style. It is a shorthand phrase, and like all shorthand terminology is subject to criticism if attention is concentrated on the words themselves rather than the concept which they are intended to designate. Nor am I particularly bothered by the fact that the phrase itself does not appear in the Constitution. Neither does the phrase "fair trial," or "freedom of association," or for that matter, "freedom of religion." Yet who would deny that these are basic concepts of our Bill of Rights? There is no magic in words; they are no more than an instrument to convey ideas. I would not be so concerned with the attack on the phrase "separation of church and state" were I not afraid that, as the phrase is simply a medium for the communication of a concept, so, too, the attack on the phrase is but a device in the attack on the concept which the phrase seeks to communicate. The attack does not come from professors of prose or masters of English style; it comes from those who are dissatisfied with the ideal with which the phrase has become associated in the American mind. Because the ideal is so precious, we must defend the phrase "separation of church and state."

In the second place, I do not find any dichotomy between the no establishment (separation) and free exercise (religious freedom) aspects of the First Amendment. There are some who say that the amendment secures two rights which are separate and of unequal value: the free-exercise right being the end, and the no-establishment the means. According to this view, when separation of church and state is (or appears to be) inconsistent with religious freedom, separation must yield to the higher good.

An illustration of the practical consequences of this argument is to be found in the claim to public funds for parochial schools. True enough, it is asserted, such use of tax-raised funds might technically be decreed a violation of the mandate of separation (though there are many who would deny even this). But refusal to allow such use interferes with the religious freedom of Catholic parents to send their children to parochial schools. Hence, the separation mandate must yield to the freedom guaranty.

I find nothing in American history to justify this dichotomy; nothing in the development of the American principle supports any justification for a division between a major and a minor premise, an end and a means. Separation and freedom are dual aspects of a single right, two sides of the same coin. The framers of the First Amendment, I believe, were committed to the proposition that freedom of religion is attainable only where separation of church and state is secure, and that the absolute separation of church and state is the best guaranty for religious freedom.

The American experiment epitomized in the First Amendment, therefore, encompasses the concept of separation of church and state as well as of freedom of worship, and deems them part of a single, unitary guaranty. I think, too, that the guaranty encompasses within its scope not only the religious but the non-religious as well. It protects Baptists as well as Episcopalians, Catholics as well as Protestants, Jews as well as Christians, and agnostics as well as believers. The same Bill of Rights that protects religious minorities protects the non-religious as well. There are not two First Amendments, one for those believing in God and the other for those who do not. Unless freedom is assured to the non-believer it can never be truly assured to the believer.

Separation and religious freedom are aspects of a dual assumption upon which our whole democracy rests. One is the assumption of voluntariness in matters of conscience and spirit, in matters of man in his relationship to God. This is as fundamental an element of the American democratic philosophy as anything can be. In no way may

a democracy coerce a person in respect to his relationship
to his Maker, in respect to his belief or lack of belief in
God. And if we accept the concept of voluntarism in matters of faith, religious association, and worship, we must
come to the ideal not only of religious freedom but of
separation of church and state. If we accept the concept
of voluntarism in matters of faith, then use of tax-raised
funds for religious schools violates the guaranty of religious freedom no less than that of separation of church
and state.

Protestants can appreciate this perhaps better than
Roman Catholics or Jews. It is difficult for many non-
Protestants to see any infringement of religious liberty in
the government's taking out of the vast public treasury
some comparatively small sum and paying it over to
parochial schools or to churches. How does this affect
the freedom of citizens? The amount so expanded can
hardly exceed a few pennies on the part of each taxpayer.
American Protestantism, however, interprets the struggle
for religious freedom largely in terms of the struggle
against taxes for religious purposes. Protestants recognize
that imposition of a tax for religious purposes constitutes
an exercise of coercion in the domain of the conscience.
They recognize too that the smallness of the tax or expenditure is immaterial; that, as Madison put it so eloquently in his great Memorial and Remonstrance against
the Virginia assessment bill, the same authority which can
force a citizen to contribute threepence only of his property for the support of religion may force him to support
any established church. Use of tax funds for religious
purposes is inconsistent with voluntarism as it is inconsistent with the separation of church and state.

The second assumption, which is equally fundamental
to our democracy and which like voluntarism in matters
of conscience distinguishes democracies from totalitarian
governments, is the assumption that the state is the servant of the people, not their master. As the creation of the
people, the state has only such powers as are delegated to
it by the people, and if it seeks to exercise a power not
delegated to it, it is guilty of despotism and tyranny.

This is the second underlying premise of democracy: the premise of limited government. It is not so in a totalitarian state; the very name totalitarian indicates that the state controls and has jurisdiction over the totality of man's life.

It may appear surprising, but in those totalitarian states behind the Iron Curtain which are committed to the ultimate destruction of religion, religion is nevertheless subsidized by the government, it is taught in the public schools, and its teachers and priests receive state salaries. In Poland, Hungary, Czechoslovakia, and Romania there has been no disavowal of Marx's assertion that religion is the opiate of the masses which must be eliminated; yet, in these countries, religion is subsidized—subsidized *and regulated*. Therein lies the explanation of the apparent paradox. In a totalitarian state nothing the people do is beyond the scope of state regulation and control. Its power encompasses the evil as well as the good. So long as religion is (deplorably) part of the people's lives, it is subject to the power and jurisdiction of the totalitarian state.

This is not so in the American democratic society. Our political government has only such powers as we give it. This is the premise of the Declaration of Independence, which expressly states that government has only those powers assigned to it by the people. This, too, is the premise of our Constitution. Equally the premise of both is that the relationship of man to God is not—and indeed cannot be, for it is inalienable—assigned to the political government.

This concept—that religion is beyond the jurisdiction of the governments of men—is the alpha and omega of our Constitution. It is the alpha, for it is implicit in the very first part of the Constitution, the Preamble, which states: "We the people of the United States in order to form a more perfect union, establish justice, insure domestic tranquility, provide for the common defense, promote the general welfare, and secure the blessings of liberty to ourselves and our posterity, do ordain and establish this Constitution for the United States of America." This Preamble sets forth the purposes for which the American government was established and the Constitution written.

Of the greatest significance is that among these expressly specified powers, conspicuously absent is any reference to a purpose of promoting religion, or worshiping God. All the purposes set forth in the Preamble concern man's relationship to man; none, to man's relationship to God. We can recognize the uniqueness of the American experiment when we realize that this was the first time in the history of at least the three major Western religions— Judaism, Christianity, and Islam—that a government, in declaring its powers and responsibilities, omitted any reference to God or religion.

This is the alpha of the Constitution. The omega is the last operative clause of the Constitution; and it states exactly the same thing. It says that there shall never be a religious test for any public office in the United States. The meanings and implications of this prohibition were well understood, both by those who framed the Constitution and those who adopted it. They all understood that it meant that the Hindu, the infidel, the Jew, even the nonbeliever in God could be a member of Congress and even President of the United States. The provision was argued, debated and finally agreed to because there was a general consensus that man's relationship to God was not and could not be the concern of the government that was being established.

These are the alpha and omega of the Constitution. And between them is the body. There, too, the experiment is manifest. Throughout the entire Constitution there is not a single reference to God. How often is it flaunted that we have "In God We Trust" on our coins. (Personally, I do not think that this marriage of God and Mammon, formalized by placing God on, of all things, money, is a great benefit either to God or to religion.) How often are we reminded that oaths of office end with the phrase "So help me God" or that "under God" is part of the Pledge of Allegiance. Yet it is never pointed out that our basic charter, the instrument from which all powers of government are derived, including the power to coin money, frame oaths of office, and provide for a pledge of allegiance, that instrument itself contains no mention of or reference to God.

This, too, was no inadvertence. The omission was a deliberate decision, made by a people launching a new experiment, a people seeking to confer upon their secular government only secular powers, and to withhold from them any powers to act in the domain of the sacred.

This experiment was not the result of any hostility to religion. On the contrary, it was predicated on a firm belief that religion prospers best when it is divorced from the political state and is inevitably corrupted when it becomes entangled with the state. Two incidents related in the Book of Kings illustrate this. One, found in II Kings, is the story of Naaman, the leper, who was the chief of staff of the king of Syria and came to Elisha to be cured of his leprosy. As he departed, he told the prophet that he always believed in the God, Jehovah, and would worship only Him. But, he continued, when he accompanied his king into the temple of Rimmon, the Syrian idol, and the king bowed to Rimmon, he too would bow. Would Elisha forgive him for this? Elisha tells him, "Go in peace." Thus we see how a person's faith is corrupted, how he engages in idolatry and practices hypocrisy, when he combines his religion with his political functions.

The second illustration is found in the first Book of Kings. The incident occurred when Jeroboam revolted against the Davidic dynasty. Jeroboam himself was a believer in Jehovah; he was no idol worshiper. Yet, in order to make sure that his people would not go to Jerusalem to worship at the Temple there, and thus perhaps re-establish their political ties with the Southern Kingdom, he built two golden calves and called upon his people to worship them as the god who brought them out of the land of Egypt. Thus he used religion to promote his political ends. The result was idolatry and the corruption of religion. This has been the history of religion throughout its existence: whenever it becomes entangled with the political state it is corrupted and the consequences are idolatry and hypocrisy.

America has given to the world a precious jewel. It has shown that a government whose concerns are purely secular and which leaves to the individual conscience of its citizenry all obligations that relate to God is the one which is actually the most friendly to religion. It is a precious jewel that we have. We should guard it well.

FREEDOM OF RELIGION VS. SEPARATION

Wilber G. Katz

My thesis is that the basic American principle of church-state relations is neither separation of church and state nor impartial benevolence toward religion; it is the principle of religious liberty, which requires strict government neutrality with respect to religion. Religion is to be kept free both from legal restraints and from government support or promotion. This principle of religious liberty is incompatible with an absolute separation of church and state. Separation is not the primary principle. The separation required by the Constitution is the separation which promotes religious liberty. The Constitution does not shrink religious liberty to the liberty which is compatible with strict separation.

This principle of strict neutrality rules out government aid to religion, however impartial. But does the federal Constitution prescribe such full neutrality or merely neutrality among religions? This question has been hotly debated in recent years and the answer is by no means clear. Both sides assume that Congress and state legislatures are forbidden to give preferential status to a particular church or religion. The controlling provision is that of the First Amendment: "Congress shall make no law respecting an establishment of religion, or prohibiting the free exercise thereof. . . ." While this prohibition applies in terms only to Congress, it has been held applicable to the states also by virtue of the due process clause of the Fourteenth Amendment. Verbally, the question thus turns on the meaning of the phrase "no law respecting an establishment of religion," but as we shall see the controlling considerations have apparently been those of an expanding American conception of religious freedom.

The question of full neutrality toward religion was not faced by the Supreme Court until 1947. In that year, the court declared that the First Amendment forbids "laws which aid one religion, aid all religions, or prefer one religion over another."[1] The amendment "requires the state to be neutral in its relation with groups of religious believers and non-believers." The case in which this interpretation was made was Everson v. Board of Education, involving the action of a New Jersey township extending to pupils in parochial schools the benefits of a bus-fare reimbursement plan. The court was unanimous in accepting the principle of "no aid to all religions," but the majority held that the principle was not violated by the bus-fare reimbursement.

Vigorous challenge met this broad interpretation of the First Amendment proscription of laws "respecting an establishment of religion." It was insisted that the clause refers only to legislation giving a preferred status to a particular religion, that the prescribed neutrality is only neutrality among religions and not between religion and non-religion. This argument was strongly pressed upon the court the following year in the case involving the Champaign, Illinois, program of "released time" religious education in public schools. Again, all the justices agreed that the amendment forbids not only preferential aid but also "impartial government assistance of all religions,"[2] although Justice Reed dissented from the holding that the program under review constituted such forbidden assistance.

In 1952, however, the court threw serious doubt upon the interpretation forbidding impartial aid to religion. The decision in Zorach v. Clauson sustained the New York released-time program, which differed from the Illinois only in that the classes in religion were not held in the public school buildings. Only the dissenting opinion of Mr. Justice Black spoke of complete neutrality and of equality

[1] Everson v. Board of Education, 330 U.S., I, 15 (1947).
[2] McCollums v. Board of Education, 333 U.S. 203, 211 (1948).

between believers and non-believers. The majority said that "When the state encourages religious instruction . . . it follows the best of our traditions." "We are a religious people whose institutions presuppose a Supreme Being."[3] To be sure, the opinion also emphasized that the Constitution "does not require the government to throw its weight against efforts to widen the effective scope of religious influence," language which is consistent with a rule of full neutrality. But the opinion's only explicit reference to neutrality is the statement that "The government must be neutral when it comes to competition between sects."[4] Mr. Justice Black accused the majority of "legal exaltation of the orthodox" and "derogation of unbelievers."[5]

In this continuing controversy before the court and in legal journals, both sides have claimed to be following "the original meaning" of the establishment clause. The evidence, however, is highly inconclusive. What the historical "studies" show primarily is that in this field of law, as in religion itself, controversy becomes so charged with emotion that objectivity is difficult to maintain.

In the first Congress, which framed the amendments incorporating the Bill of Rights, several of the early drafts of the "establishment" clause forbade only laws establishing a particular church. The version adopted by the Senate was of this type, although the draft approved in the House had been more general, covering laws "establishing religion." There is little evidence of the intention of the conference committee which reported the final language: "no law respecting an establishment of religion," although this language was apparently insisted upon by members of the House. Those who support the broad interpretation of this language usually agree that it was intended to incorporate the views expressed by James Madison in 1785 in his Memorial and Remonstrance Against Religious Assessments. This document was an elaborately reasoned argument against a bill in the Virginia legislature to levy a tax for the support of "Teachers of

[3] Ibid., at pp. 313–314.
[4] Ibid.
[5] 343 U.S. at p. 319 (1952).

the Christian Religion." Taxpayers were to have the privilege of designating the particular "society of Christians" to which this tax should be paid, and for those who preferred to make no such designation the tax proceeds were to be applied by the legislature "for the encouragement of seminaries of learning." This important document and the bill to which it was addressed were incorporated in full in appendices to Mr. Justice Rutledge's opinion in the New Jersey bus case.[6]

Madison's remonstrance eloquently defended the position that religion should be entirely free from state aid. It is by no means clear however, that Madison himself urged that this principle should be incorporated in the federal Bill of Rights. The draft amendment introduced by Madison used the language "nor shall any national religion be established . . ."[7] At the time at least five of the states still gave preferential status to particular churches, and it seems clear that Congress was to have neither the power to choose among them nor the power to abolish such "establishments." This may, indeed, be the only intention reflected in the choice of the language "no law respecting an establishment of religion."

As already noted, the First Amendment limitations upon congressional power have been held extended to the states by the Fourteenth Amendment provision that no person shall be deprived of liberty without due process of law. It is understandable that the court should have subsumed under the term "liberty" the freedoms of speech, press, assembly, and petition covered by the First Amendment and also the "free exercise of religion." However, the court might well have found more difficulty in thus "incorporating" in the due-process clause the prohibition of laws "respecting an establishment of religion." It is paradoxical that a clause the terms of which protected state-established churches from congressional action should come to mean that no state may have an established church. On the other hand, when the Fourteenth Amendment was adopted, no

[6] Everson *v.* Board of Education, 330 U.S. at pp. 63–74.
[7] United States Congress, *Annals*, Washington, 1834, I, 434.

established churches, in the ordinary sense, remained, although some states still had provisions discriminating against non-Christians. The liberty protected by the Fourteenth Amendment might then have been understood as including freedom from church establishment, but it could hardly have been understood more broadly as making religion free from all discrimination and even from non-discriminatory state aid.

The American conception of religious freedom has continued to expand, however, and in many areas the Supreme Court has given expanding scope to constitutional liberties. It would not, therefore, be surprising if the mature American concept of religious liberty should come to preclude not only preferential treatment of a particular religion, but all exertion of government influence in favor of religion, however impartial. Religious liberty would thus include freedom to doubt on a full parity with freedom to believe.

Much of the opposition to this view apparently springs from a fear that strict government neutrality would mean, in effect, hostility to religion. This is because strict neutrality is often confused with strict separation of church and state. It is important to keep these concepts separate and to see neutrality as the controlling concept. If the state is to be neutral, it cannot be insulated from contact with religion. Many types of government provision for religion are necessary under the strict neutrality principle in order to avoid unintended restraints upon religious freedom. For example, provision for voluntary worship in the armed forces is constitutional, not because government policy may properly favor religion, but because, in the absence of some provision for worship, the government would be exercising its military powers in a manner hostile to religious freedom. The government is not required to abandon neutrality in an effort to maintain strict separation.

As government activity is extended, instances multiply where strict separation would limit religious freedom and where action which might appear as government aid is only the result of an effort to maintain full neutrality. A recent instance is furnished by the urban renewal project for the Lincoln Square area in New York. In the plan two blocks were set aside for educational purposes, and Fordham University was permitted to acquire this property from the city at $7 per square foot, less than half of the estimated cost. Objections that this constituted aid to sectarian education were overruled. Justice McGivern said, "To hold, under the instant circumstances, that a denominational school may not be afforded the same opportunity to contract as any other private institution or corporation, would be to convert the constitutional safeguards into a sword against the freedoms which they were intended to shield."[8]

The exemptions from property taxation usually granted to churches and religious charities are often cited as showing that non-discriminatory aid to religion is permissible. Such exemptions, furthermore, have been opposed by advocates of the "no aid" principle. The typical exemptions, however, apply not only to religious bodies but to a general class of non-profit organizations including non-religious schools and charities. Inclusion of religious bodies in such a general exemption is defensible as an effort to maintain neutrality and avoid discrimination against religion. Only if churches were singled out for a special exemption would the question of the propriety of affirmative aid to religion be squarely presented.

Some writers have supported "co-operation" between church and state, using language which seems to suggest more freedom for state aid than strict neutrality would permit. Thus Alexander Meiklejohn has urged that the state and the churches have a community of interest in education which requires active co-operation. He insists that a democracy is concerned that its citizens find living roots for democratic attitudes and for faith in the possibility of responsible self-government. Since "40 or 50 or 60 per cent of our people" find in religious beliefs the ultimate

---

[8] 173 N.Y.S. 2d at p. 703. Compare the language of the Court of Appeals: "Special Term pointed out, probably correctly, that Fordham would be deprived of constitutional rights if it alone were excluded from the bidding."

moral ground for democratic institutions, a democracy should give to a religious belief a "positive status in the public planning of education."[9] But this positive status he asks equally for non-religious efforts to teach respect for the human spirit and its freedom. Thus the co-operation which Meiklejohn approves is the co-operation of a positive neutrality which is careful to avoid undermining the effective freedom of religious teaching.

Similarly, John C. Bennett distinguishes between aid to all religions for their own sake ("multiple establishment") and the "co-operation" or aid which is necessary to the "free exercise" of religion. Where "the state finds itself involved in activities, such as education, in which the churches have a special stake . . . it may . . . seek to arrive at some adjustment that limits the injury to the interests for which the churches stand."[10]

The competition between the principles of separation and neutrality is most sharply illustrated in the hotly debated issue of the application of tax funds to educational costs in parochial schools. This aspect raises serious legal questions. The central question, as it relates to the power of Congress, may be considered in the context of a section of the United States Code that is seldom noticed. This is the provision made by Congress for the education of the pages who serve in the houses of Congress and in the Supreme Court. Funds are appropriated to the school authorities of the District of Columbia to cover the cost of instruction of the pages attending the public schools. For those choosing to attend a parochial or private school, payment is directed to be made to the school chosen (but at a rate no higher than paid for public school education). This statute was apparently enacted without opposition. Is it open to constitutional attack as a "law respecting an establishment of religion"? Could Congress make similar provision for other children living in the District? Would it be permissible for a state to divide tax money on a

[9] Ibid., pp. 62, 67.
[10] John C. Bennett, *Christians and the State* (New York, 1958), p. 233.

similar principle between patrons of public and private schools?

In discussions of such questions, it is usually agreed that parents may not be required to send their children to public schools. This was decided unanimously by the Supreme Court in 1925 in Pierce *v.* Society of Sisters. The Oregon statute under review was held to deprive parents and children of "liberty" in violation of the Fourteenth Amendment. Since the case was decided before the court had come to speak of the Fourteenth Amendment as "incorporating" the First, no reference was made to the First Amendment guaranty of "free exercise of religion." Very rarely is it urged that this decision should be overruled, but as one reads discussions of the tax-support problem, one gets the impression that many people concede only reluctantly that the Constitution protects in this way the freedom to combine secular and religious education.

The defense of the type of financial provision illustrated in the page-boy statute is based explicitly on the Pierce case. If parents have a right to choose a parochial school, presumably this choice should be free from discriminatory burdens. At least it should be permissible for the government to arrange its tax and school policies so as to avoid such discrimination. This is the theory on which, in many states, parochial school pupils are included in arrangements for free bus transportation. In sustaining the validity of such inclusion, Mr. Justice Black said for the majority of the court: ". . . we must be careful in protecting the citizens of New Jersey against state-established churches, to be sure that we do not inadvertently prohibit New Jersey from extending its general State law benefits to all its citizens without regard to their religious beliefs."[11]

The classic statement of the strict separation position is that of Mr. Justice Rutledge's dissenting opinion in this case. He used the arresting metaphor of a price exacted by the Constitution for religious liberty. "Like St. Paul's freedom religious liberty with a great price must be

[11] Everson *v.* Board of Education, 330 U.S., I, 16 (1947).

bought. And for those who exercise it most fully, by insisting upon religious education for their children mixed with secular, by the terms of our Constitution the price is greater than for others."[12] The "price" includes surrender of any share in the tax funds applied to educational costs or to "fringe" items such as bus transportation. This price tag Mr. Justice Rutledge found in the phrase "no law respecting an establishment of religion" which he construed as requiring a complete and permanent separation of religious activity and civil authority.

This reasoning would make invalid the page-boy statute and also the veterans' education provisions of the G.I. Bill of Rights. Under these provisions, veterans might choose to have the payments applied to tuition in church-related colleges or even in sectarian schools for training of ministers. This precedent is not to be distinguished as dealing merely with compensation for services rendered the government. It does not involve compensation which the recipient is free to spend for purposes other than education. When the question relates to educational costs awarded to government employees as additional compensation, there is no greater justification for abandoning church-state separation and permitting the government to respect religious preferences than where the question relates to educational costs for citizens generally.

I have contended that the basic principle embodied in the religion clause of the First Amendment is the principle of strict neutrality, leaving religion free from government discrimination against it or in its favor. In my opinion, this principle supports not only measures like the G.I. Bill, the page-boy statute, and non-discriminatory school bus plans, but also inclusion of parochial schools in the application of tax funds to the cost of instruction in secular subjects. The almost universal rejection of this view by non-Catholics represents a denial of full religious liberty and reflects hostility to parochial schools and perhaps fear of the extension of the political influence of a clerical hierarchy.

[12] Everson v. Board of Education, 330 U.S. 28, 59 (1947).

Such a curtailment of religious liberty would be expected if one were to accept the suggestion of Professor Mark DeWolfe Howe that the American doctrine of religious liberty has theological presuppositions which are inconsistent with full neutrality among religious groups. He says that we shall not reach the heart of our constitutional problem until we ask "whether the objective of freedom and separation is not so intimately related to an article of religious faith as to make the state a religious partisan when it seeks to attain that objective."[13] "Those who support the thesis that each man should be left free by government to follow the faith which his mind and heart prefer, very generally, if not invariably, have in religion, abandoned the belief that an ultimate truth has been revealed for all and, as truth, is binding on all. The political conviction that religious liberty is of profound importance generally bespeaks a Protestant, and very frequently a skeptical attitude towards the 'truths' of religion. Behind our constitutional provisions there may lie, therefore, an attitude, if not a religious faith itself, which is predominantly Protestant in spirit."[14]

Howe concludes that "It is unlikely that the equality which results from liberty will be attained by any church which is committed, or seems to the bulk of the community to be committed, to the doctrine not only that all men are obligated to seek and follow the truth, but that the truth is to be found in its faith only. This is not because civil government as such is unwilling to perform the political promise contained in constitutions but because performance would entail the violation of religious presuppositions in which the promise is grounded."[15]

This is an interpretation of the Constitution that I would have the greatest reluctance to accept. It is reminiscent of the late pressures to deny freedom of speech and assembly to those whose ideas are hostile to basic American

[13] Mark DeWolfe Howe, review of Anson Phelps Stokes, *Church and State in the United States, Harvard Law Review,* LXIV, November 1950, pp. 170, 175.

[14] Ibid., p. 172.

[15] Ibid., pp. 172–173.

liberties. Notwithstanding these pressures, the courts have usually heeded Mr. Justice Holmes's reminder that freedom of thought includes "freedom for the thought that we hate."

So far we have dealt with the problem as though only the federal Constitution were involved. In many states, however, the state constitution provides an additional obstacle. This is in the form of an explicit provision forbidding (in varying language) any use of tax funds for the support of sectarian schools. A few state courts have given such provisions a narrow construction. Thus, in Illinois, payments to sectarian industrial schools in amounts not exceeding the cost of the service furnished have been held not "grants" to the schools. This reasoning, however, if applied to ordinary parochial schools, would leave little scope to such prohibitions. In view of the history of their adoption during the nineteenth-century controversies over parochial schools, the general application of this narrow construction would seem unwarranted. In many states, furthermore, the provisions have been broadly construed from the outset. Even if the future should see the disappearance of hostility to parochial schools, the abolition of financial discrimination against their patrons would in many states have to await amendment of the state constitution. Under provisions as specific as these, there is less room for evolution of constitutional law by judicial interpretation than in the case of vague words such as "liberty" and "establishment."

American religious freedom is subject, of course, to many other limitations. Legislation may validly forbid some types of conduct which a particular religion deems obligatory, or may prescribe action forbidden by religious law. Some such limitations are obviously necessary to protect the interests of citizens who do not share the particular faith. This justification may cover measures such as compulsory vaccination and isolation of victims of contagious disease. The restrictions, however, are often more broadly defined and seem designed to give to the faithful themselves a protection they do not wish. Thus prohibitions of ceremonial use of poisonous snakes are not limited to their use in services which are attended by outsiders.

Sometimes a legal requirement is made applicable only to children, overruling religious convictions of parents, such as those against blood transfusion or against medical treatment in general.

Limitations on the free exercise of religion are not lightly to be imposed, however; they can be justified only in terms of "grave and immediate danger to interests which the state may lawfully protect" (language quoted from the opinion holding that children of Jehovah's Witnesses must be excused from a compulsory flag salute regulation).

As one reflects upon the limits of constitutional religious liberty, it may be suggestive to contrast our permissive policy toward conscientious objectors with our strict prohibition of plural marriage. Congress is not constitutionally required to respect religious scruples as to military service, and the exemption of conscientious objectors is widely hailed as showing the strength of American traditions and freedom. On the other hand, our historic policy of suppression of Mormon marriage institutions is almost taken for granted. Perhaps we should at least ask whether the compulsion is applied for the good of the Saints themselves or whether it is the public peace or stability of gentile monogamy which would be threatened by a toleration of deviant marriage customs. In any event we must remember this chapter of our continuing history lest we claim too wide a scope for American religious liberty.

Legal problems of American religious conflict can best be viewed as problems of conflicting freedoms. These freedoms include the conflicting freedoms of secular humanists and believers in God. They include not only religious freedom but other civil liberties, whose maintenance—in Justice Rutledge's candid language—may require that a price be exacted for the exercise of religious freedom. Justice Frankfurter characterized the secular public school as a means of reconciling freedom in general with religious freedom. If all these freedoms were properly defined, perhaps they would not be in conflict. Perhaps conflict arises only because it is forgotten that religious freedom, like other freedoms, is responsible freedom, and that each of us has a religious stake in the religious freedom of others. Wide support for legislation extending religious freedom can be expected only when citizens believe that the groups which ask for freedom can be trusted to follow the principle that all religion should be free.

THE SUPREME COURT ON
CHURCH AND STATE

I

[From the majority opinion in Everson *v.* Board of Education (1946), where it was held constitutional for the state of New Jersey to provide tax funds for parochial school transportation. In the course of this opinion, based finally on "child welfare" grounds, the majority of the Court expressed some basic thoughts on the meaning of the establishment clause.]

The "establishment of religion" clause of the First Amendment means at least this: Neither a state nor the Federal Government can set up a church. Neither can pass laws which aid one religion, aid all religions, or prefer one religion over another. Neither can force nor influence a person to go to or remain away from church against his will or force him to profess a belief or disbelief in any religion. No person can be punished for entertaining or professing religious beliefs or disbeliefs, for church attendance or non-attendance. No tax in any amount, large or small, can be levied to support any religious activities or institutions, whatever they may be called, or whatever form they may adopt to teach or practice religion. Neither a state nor the Federal Government can, openly or secretly, participate in the affairs of any religious organizations or groups and vice versa. In the words of Jefferson the clause against establishment of religion by law was intended to erect "a wall of separation between Church and State."

We must consider the New Jersey statute in accordance with the foregoing limitations imposed by the First Amendment. But we must not strike that State statute down if it is within the State's constitutional power even though it approaches the verge of the power. New Jersey cannot consistently with the "establishment of religion clause" of the First Amendment contribute tax-raised funds to the support of an institution which teaches the tenets and faith of any church. On the other hand other language of the amendment commands that New Jersey cannot hamper its citizens in the free exercise of their own religion. Consequently, it cannot exclude individual Catholics, Lutherans, Mohammedans, Baptists, Jews, Methodists, Non-believers, Presbyterians, or the members of any other faith, *because of their faith, or lack of it,* from receiving the benefits of public welfare legislation. While we do not mean to intimate that a state could not provide transportation only to children attending public schools, we must be careful, in protecting the citizens of New Jersey against state-established churches, to be sure that we do not inadvertently prohibit New Jersey from extending its general State law benefits to all its citizens without regard to their religious belief.

Measured by these standards, we cannot say that the First Amendment prohibits New Jersey from spending tax-raised funds to pay the bus fares of parochial school pupils as a part of a general program under which it pays the fares of pupils attending public and other schools. It is undoubtedly true that children are helped to get to church schools. There is even a possibility that some of the children might not be sent to the church schools if the parents were compelled to pay their children's bus fares out of their own pockets when transportation to a public school would have been paid for by the state. The same possibility exists where the state requires a local transit company to provide reduced fares to school children including those attending parochial schools, or where a municipally owned transportation system undertakes to carry all school children free of charge. Moreover, state-paid policemen, detailed to protect children going to and from church schools from the very real hazards of traffic, would serve much the same purpose and accomplish much the same result as state provisions intended to guarantee free transportation of a kind which the state deems to be best for the school children's welfare. And parents might refuse to risk their children to the serious danger of traffic accidents going to and from parochial schools, the approaches to which were not protected by policemen. Similarly, parents might be reluctant to permit their children to attend schools which the state had cut off from such general government services as ordinary police and fire protection, connections for sewage disposal, public highways and sidewalks. Of course, cutting off church schools from these services, so separate and so indisputably marked off from the religious function, would make it far more difficult for the schools to operate. But such is obviously not the purpose of the First Amendment. That Amendment requires the state to be a neutral in its relations with groups of religious believers and non-believers; it does not require the state to be their adversary. State power is no more to be used so as to handicap religions than it is to favor them.

This Court has said that parents may, in the discharge of their duty under state compulsory education laws, send their children to a religious rather than a public school if the school meets the secular educational requirements which the state has power to impose. It appears that these parochial schools meet New Jersey's requirements. The State contributes no money to the schools. It does not support them. Its legislation, as applied, does no more than provide a general program to help parents get their children, regardless of their religion, safely and expeditiously to and from accredited schools.

The First Amendment has erected a wall between church and state. That wall must be kept high and impregnable. We could not approve the slightest breach. New Jersey has not breached it here.

II

[From the minority opinion in Everson *v.* Board of Education. The minority was sizable, consisting of four Justices who argued that tax support for parochial school transportation is illegal.]

No one conscious of religious values can be unsympathetic toward the burden which our constitutional separation puts on parents who desire religious instruction mixed with secular for their children. They pay taxes for others' children's education, at the same time the added cost of instruction for their own. Nor can one happily see benefits denied to children which others receive, because in conscience they or their parents for them desire a different kind of training others do not demand.

But if those feelings should prevail, there would be an end to our historic constitutional policy and command. No more unjust or discriminatory in fact is it to deny attendants at religious schools the cost of their transportation than it is to deny them tuitions, sustenance for their teachers, or any other educational expense which others receive at public cost. Hardship in fact there is which none can blink. But, for assuring to those who undergo it the greater, the most comprehensive freedom, it is one written by design and firm intent into our basic law.

Of course discrimination in the legal sense does not exist. The child attending the religious school has the same right as any other to attend the public school. But he foregoes exercising it because the same guaranty which assures this freedom forbids the public school or any agency of the state to give or aid him in securing the religious instruction he seeks.

Were he to accept the common school, he would be the first to protest the teaching there of any creed or faith not his own. And it is precisely for the reason that their atmosphere is wholly secular that children are not sent to public schools under the *Pierce* doctrine. But that is a constitutional necessity, because we have staked the very existence of our country on the faith that complete separation between the state and religion is best for the state and best for religion.

That policy necessarily entails hardship upon persons who forego the right to educational advantages the state can supply in order to secure others it is precluded from giving. Indeed this may hamper the parent and the child forced by conscience to that choice. But it does not make the state unneutral to withhold what the Constitution forbids it to give. On the contrary it is only by observing the prohibition rigidly that the state can maintain its neutrality and avoid partisanship in the dissensions inevitable when sect opposes sect over demands for public moneys to further religious education, teaching or training in any form or degree, directly or indirectly. Like St. Paul's freedom, religious liberty with a great price must be bought. And for those who exercise it most fully, by insisting upon religious education for their children mixed with secular, by the terms of our Constitution the price is greater than for others.

The problem then cannot be cast in terms of legal discrimination or its absence. This would be true, even though the state in giving aid should treat all religious instruction alike. Thus, if the present statute and its application were shown to apply equally to all religious schools of whatever faith, yet in the light of our tradition it could not stand. For then the adherent of one creed still would pay for the support of another, the childless taxpayer with others more fortunate. Then too there would seem to be no bar to making appropriations for transportation and other expenses of children attending public or other secular schools, after hours in separate places and classes for their exclusively religious instruction. The person who embraces no creed also would be forced to pay for teaching what he does not believe. Again, it was the furnishing of "contributions of money for the propagation of opinions which he disbelieves" that the fathers outlawed. That consequence and effect are not removed by multiplying to all-inclusiveness the sects for which support is exacted. The Constitution requires, not comprehensive identification of state with religion, but complete separation.

Whatever might be said of some other application of New Jersey's statute, the one made here has no semblance of bearing as a safety measure, or indeed, for securing expeditious conveyance. The transportation supplied is by public conveyance, subject to all the hazards and delays of the highway and the streets incurred by the public generally in going about its multifarious business.

Nor is the case comparable to one of furnishing fire or police protection, or access to public highways. These things are matters of common right, part of the general need for safety. Certainly the fire department must not stand idly by while the church burns. Nor is this reason why the state should pay the expense of transportation or other items of the cost of religious education.

Two great drives are constantly in motion to abridge, in the name of education, the complete division of religion and civil authority which our forefathers made. One is to introduce religious education and observances into the public schools. The other, to obtain public funds for the aid and support of various private religious schools. In my opinion both avenues were closed by the Constitution. Neither should be opened by this Court. The matter is not one of quantity, to be measured by the amount of money expended. Now as in Madison's day it is one of principle, to keep separate the separate spheres as the First Amendment drew them; to prevent the first experiment upon liberties; and to keep the question from becoming entangled in corrosive precedents. We should not be less strict to keep strong and untarnished the one side of the shield of religious freedom than we have been of the other.

III

[From the majority opinion in McCollum v. Board of Education (1948), where it was held unconstitutional for "released time" programs to be held on school grounds. Under that program, children whose parents consented were released from the regular school schedule for thirty or forty-five minutes once a week, so that they could attend religious classes under the auspices of their own church or synagogue. These classes were held on school property.]

The . . . facts show the use of tax-supported property for religious instruction and the close cooperation between the school authorities and the religious council in promoting religious education. The operation of the state's compulsory education system thus assists and is integrated with the program of religious instruction carried on by separate religious sects. Pupils compelled by law to go to school for secular education are released in part from their legal duty upon the condition that they attend the religious classes. This is beyond all question a utilization of the tax-established and tax-supported public school system to aid religious groups to spread their faith. And it falls squarely under the ban of the First Amendment (made applicable to the States by the Fourteenth) as we interpreted it in *Everson v. Board of Education.* There we said: "Neither a state nor the Federal Government can set up a church. Neither can pass laws which aid one religion, aid all religions, or prefer one religion over another. Neither can force or influence a person to go to or to remain away from church against his will or force him to profess a belief or disbelief in any religion. No person can be punished for entertaining or for professing religious beliefs or disbeliefs, for church attendance or nonattendance. No tax in any amount, large or small, can be levied to support any religious activities or institutions, whatever they may be called, or whatever form they may adopt to teach or practice religion. Neither a state nor the Federal Government can, openly or secretly, participate in the affairs of any religious organizations or groups, and *vice versa.* In the words of Jefferson, the clause against establishment of religion by law was intended to erect 'a wall of separation between Church and State.'" Ibid. at 15–16. The majority in the *Everson* case, and the minority . . . agreed that the First Amendment's language, properly interpreted, had erected a wall of separation between Church and State . . .

To hold that a state cannot consistently with the First

and Fourteenth Amendments utilize its public school system to aid any or all religious faiths or sects in the dissemination of their doctrines and ideals does not, as counsel urges, manifest a governmental hostility to religion or religious teachings. A manifestation of such hostility would be at war with our national tradition as embodied in the First Amendment's guaranty of the free exercise of religion. For the First Amendment rests upon the premise that both religion and government can best work to achieve their lofty aims if each is left free from the other within its respective sphere. Or, as we said in the *Everson* case, the First Amendment has erected a wall between Church and State which must be kept high and impregnable.

Here not only are the state's tax-supported public school buildings used for the dissemination of religious doctrines. The State also affords sectarian groups an invaluable aid in that it helps to provide pupils for their religious classes through use of the state's compulsory public school machinery. This is not separation of Church and State.

IV

[From the majority opinion in Zorach *v*. Clauson (1952) where released-time programs which were *not* conducted on school property were held constitutional. Justice Black dissented from the majority opinion, commenting: "Before today, our judicial opinions have refrained from drawing invidious distinctions between those who believe in no religion and those who do believe. The First Amendment has lost much if the religious follower and the atheist are no longer to be judicially regarded as entitled to equal justice under law."]

This "released time" program involves neither religious instruction in public school classrooms nor the expenditure of public funds. All costs, including the application blanks, are paid by the religious organizations. The case is therefore unlike McCollum v. Board of Education which involved a "released time" program from Illinois. In that case the classrooms were turned over to religious instructors. We accordingly held that the program violated the First Amendment which (by reason of the Fourteenth Amendment) prohibits the states from establishing religion or prohibiting its free exercise.

It takes obtuse reasoning to inject any issue of the "free exercise" of religion into the present case. No one is forced to go to the religious classroom and no religious exercise or instruction is brought to the classrooms of the public schools. A student need not take religious instruction. He is left to his own desires as to the manner or time of his religious devotions, if any.

There is a suggestion that the system involves the use of coercion to get public school students into religious classrooms. There is no evidence in the record before us that supports that conclusion. The present record indeed tells us that the school authorities are neutral in this regard and do no more than release students whose parents so request. If in fact coercion were used, if it were established that any one or more teachers were using their office to persuade or force students to take the religious instruction, a wholly different case would be presented. Hence we put aside that claim of coercion both as respects the "free exercise" of religion and "an establishment of religion" within the meaning of the First Amendment.

Moreover, apart from that claim of coercion, we do not see how New York by this type of "released time" program has made a law respecting an establishment of religion within the meaning of the First Amendment. There is much talk of the separation of Church and State in the history of the Bill of Rights and in the decisions clustering around the First Amendment. See Everson v. Board of Education; McCollum v. Board of Education. There cannot be the slightest doubt that the First Amendment reflects the philosophy that Church and State should be separated. And so far as interference with the "free exercise" of religion and an "establishment" of religion are concerned, the separation must be complete and unequivocal. The First Amendment within the scope of its coverage permits no exception; the prohibition is absolute. The First Amendment, however, does not say that in every and all respects there shall be a separation of Church and State. Rather, it studiously defines the manner, the specific ways, in which there shall be no concert or union or dependency one on the other. That is the common sense of the matter. Otherwise the state and religion would be aliens to each other—hostile, suspicious, and even unfriendly. Churches could not be required to pay even property taxes. Municipalities would not be permitted to render police or fire protection to religious groups. Policemen who helped parishioners into their places of worship would violate the Constitution. Prayers in our legislative halls; the appeals to the Almighty in the messages of the Chief Executive; the proclamations making Thanksgiving Day a holiday; "so help me God" in our courtroom oaths —these and all other references to the Almighty that run through our laws, our public rituals, our ceremonies would be flouting the First Amendment. A fastidious atheist or agnostic could even object to the supplication with which the Court opens each session: "God save the United States and this Honorable Court."

We would have to press the concept of separation of Church and State to these extremes to condemn the present law on constitutional grounds. The nullification of this law would have wide and profound effects. A Catholic student applies to his teacher for permission to leave the school during hours on a Holy Day of Obligation to attend a mass. A Jewish student asks his teacher for permission to be excused for Yom Kippur. A Protestant wants the afternoon off for a family baptismal ceremony. In each case the teacher requires parental consent in writing. In each case the teacher, in order to make sure the student is not a truant, goes further and requires a report from the priest, the rabbi, or the minister. The teacher in other words cooperates in a religious program to the extent of making it possible for her students to participate in it. Whether she does it occasionally for a few students, regularly for one, or pursuant to a systematized program designed to further the religious needs of all the students does not alter the character of the act.

We are a religious people whose institutions presuppose a Supreme Being. We guarantee the freedom to worship as one chooses. We make room for as wide a variety of beliefs and creeds as the spiritual needs of man deem necessary. We sponsor an attitude on the part of government that shows no partiality to any one group and that lets each flourish according to the zeal of its adherents and the appeal of its dogma. When the state encourages religious instruction or cooperates with religious authorities by adjusting the schedule of public events to sectarian needs, it follows the best of our traditions. For it then respects the religious nature of our people and accommodates the public service to their spiritual needs. To hold that it may not would be to find in the Constitution a requirement that the government show a callous indifference to religious groups. That would be preferring those who believe in no religion over those who do believe. Government may not finance religious groups nor undertake religious instruction nor blend secular and sectarian education nor use secular institutions to force one or some religion on any person. But we find no constitutional requirement which makes it necessary for government to be hostile to religion and to throw its weight against efforts to widen the effective scope of religious influence. The government must be neutral when it comes to competition between sects. It may not thrust any sect on any person. It may not make a religious observance compulsory. It may not coerce anyone to attend church, to observe a religious holiday, or to take religious instruction. But it can close its doors or suspend its operations as to those who want to repair to their religious sanctuary for worship or instruction. No more than that is undertaken here.

This program may be unwise and improvident from an educational or a community viewpoint. That appeal is made to us on a theory, previously advanced, that each case must be decided on the basis of "our own prepossessions." See McCollum v. Board of Education. Our individual preferences, however, are not the constitutional standard. The constitutional standard is the separation of Church and State. The problem, like many problems in constitutional law, is one of degree.

V

[From the majority opinion in Engel *v.* Vitale (1961) in which a prayer devised by the New York State Board of Regents for recital by public school classes at the beginning of each day was held unconstitutional. The prayer, designed to be "non-sectarian," read: "Almighty God, we acknowledge our dependence upon Thee, and we beg Thy blessings upon us, our parents, our teachers and our country." Students could be excused from this recitation on request of their parents.]

We think that by using its public school system to encourage recitation of the Regents' prayer, the State of New York has adopted a practice wholly inconsistent with the Establishment Clause. There can, of course, be no doubt that New York's program of daily classroom invocation of God's blessings as prescribed in the Regents' prayer is a religious activity. It is a solemn avowal of divine faith and supplication for the blessings of the Almighty. The nature of such a prayer has always been religious, none of the respondents has denied this and the trial court expressly so found:

> The religious nature of prayer was recognized by Jefferson and has been concurred in by theological writers, the United States Supreme Court and State Courts and administrative officials, including New York's Commissioner of Education. A committee of the New York Legislature has agreed.

> The Board of Regents as *amicus curiae,* the respondents and intervenors all concede the religious nature of prayer, but seek to distinguish this prayer because it is based on our spiritual heritage. . . .

The petitioners contend among other things that the state laws requiring or permitting use of the Regents' prayer must be struck down as a violation of the Establishment Clause because that prayer was composed by governmental officials as a part of a governmental program to further religious beliefs. For this reason, petitioners argue, the State's use of the Regents' prayer in its public school system breaches the constitutional wall of separation between Church and State. We agree with that contention since we think that the constitutional prohibition against laws respecting an establishment of religion must at least mean that in this country it is no part of the business of government to compose official prayers for any group of the American people to recite as a part of a religious program carried on by government.

By the time of the adoption of the Constitution, our history shows that there was a widespread awareness among many Americans of the dangers of a union of Church and State. These people knew, some of them from bitter personal experience, that one of the greatest dangers to the freedom of the individual to worship in his own way lay in the Government's placing its official stamp of approval upon one particular kind of prayer or one particular form of religious services. They knew the anguish, hardship and bitter strife that could come when zealous religious groups struggled with one another to obtain the Government's stamp of approval from each King, Queen, or Protector that came to temporary power. The Constitution was intended to avert a part of this danger by leaving the government of this country in the hands of the people rather than in the hands of any monarch. But this safeguard was not enough. Our Founders were no more willing to let the content of their prayers and their privilege of praying whenever they pleased be influenced by the ballot box than they were to let these vital matters of personal conscience depend upon the succession of monarchs. The First Amendment was added to the Constitution to stand as a guarantee that neither the power nor the prestige of the

Federal Government would be used to control, support or influence the kinds of prayer the American people can say —that the people's religions must not be subjected to the pressures of government for change each time a new political administration is elected to office. Under that Amendment's prohibition against governmental establishment of religion, as reinforced by the provisions of the Fourteenth Amendment, government in this country, be it state or federal, is without power to prescribe by law any particular form of prayer which is to be used as an official prayer in carrying on any program of governmentally sponsored religious activity.

There can be no doubt that New York's state prayer program officially establishes the religious beliefs embodied in the Regents' prayer. The respondents' argument to the contrary, which is largely based upon the contention that the Regents' prayer is "non-denominational" and the fact that the program, as modified and approved by state courts, does not require all pupils to recite the prayer but permits those who wish to do so to remain silent or be excused from the room, ignores the essential nature of the program's constitutional defects. Neither the fact that the prayer may be denominationally neutral, nor the fact that its observance on the part of the students is voluntary can serve to free it from the limitations of the Establishment Clause, as it might from the Free Exercise Clause, of the First Amendment, both of which are operative against the States by virtue of the Fourteenth Amendment. Although these two clauses may in certain instances overlap, they forbid two quite different kinds of governmental encroachment upon religious freedom. The Establishment Clause, unlike the Free Exercise Clause, does not depend upon any showing of direct governmental compulsion and is violated by the enactment of laws which establish an official religion whether those laws operate directly to coerce nonobserving individuals or not. This is not to say, of course, that laws officially prescribing a particular form of religious worship do not involve coercion of such individuals. When the power, prestige and financial support of government is placed behind a particular religious belief, the indirect coercive pressure upon religious minorities to conform to the prevailing officially approved religion is plain. But the purposes underlying the Establishment Clause go much further than that. Its first and most immediate purpose rested on the belief that a union of government and religion tends to destroy government and to degrade religion. The history of governmentally established religion, both in England and in this country, showed that whenever government had allied itself with one particular form of religion, the inevitable result had been that it had incurred the hatred, disrespect and even contempt of those who held contrary beliefs. That same history showed that many people had lost their respect for any religion that had relied upon the support of government to spread its faith. The Establishment Clause thus stands as an expression of principle on the part of the Founders of our Constitution that religion is too personal, too sacred, too holy, to permit its "unhallowed perversion" by a civil magistrate.

It is true that New York's establishment of its Regents' prayer as an officially approved religious doctrine of that State does not amount to a total establishment of one particular religious sect to the exclusion of all others—that, indeed, the governmental endorsement of that prayer seems relatively insignificant when compared to the governmental encroachments upon religion which were commonplace 200 years ago. To those who may subscribe to the view that because the Regents' official prayer is so brief and general there can be no danger to religious freedom in its governmental establishment, however, it may be appropriate to say in the words of James Madison, the author of the First Amendment:

It is proper to take alarm at the first experiment on our liberties. . . . Who does not see that the same authority which can establish Christianity, in exclusion of all other religions, may establish with the same ease any particular sect of Christians in exclusion of all other sects? That the same authority which can force a citizen to contribute three pence only of his property for the support of any one establishment, may force him to conform to any other establishment in all cases whatsoever?

VI

[From the minority opinion in Engel *v.* Vitale, as expressed by the lone dissenter, Justice Stewart.]

The Court does not hold, nor could it, that New York has interfered with the free exercise of anybody's religion. For the state courts have made clear that those who object to reciting the prayer must be entirely free of any compulsion to do so, including any "embarrassments and pressures." But the Court says that in permitting school children to say this simple prayer, the New York authorities have established "an official religion."

With all respect, I think the Court has misapplied a great constitutional principle. I cannot see how an "official religion" is established by letting those who want to say prayer say it. On the contrary, I think that to deny the wish of these school children to join in reciting this prayer is to deny them the opportunity of sharing in the spiritual heritage of our Nation.

The Court's historical review of the quarrels over the Book of Common Prayer in England throws no light for me on the issue before us in this case. England had then and has now an established church. Equally unenlightening, I think, is the history of the early establishment and later rejection of an official church in our own States. For we deal here not with the establishment of a state church, which would, of course, be constitutionally impermissible, but with whether school children who want to begin their day by joining in prayer must be prohibited from doing so. Moreover, I think that the Court's task, in this as in all areas of constitutional adjudication, is not responsibly aided by the uncritical invocation of metaphors like the "wall of separation," a phrase nowhere to be found in the Constitution. What is relevant to the issue here is not the history of an established church in sixteenth century England or in eighteenth century America, but the history of the religious traditions of our people, reflected in countless practices of the institutions and officials of our government.

At the opening of each day's Session of this Court we stand, while one of our officials invokes the protection of God. Since the days of John Marshall our Crier has said, "God save the United States and this Honorable Court." Both the Senate and the House of Representatives open their daily Sessions with prayer. Each of our Presidents, from George Washington to John F. Kennedy, has upon assuming his Office asked the protection and help of God.

The Court today says that the state and federal governments are without constitutional power to prescribe any particular form of words to be recited by any group of the American people on any subject touching religion. The third stanza of "The Star-Spangled Banner," made our National Anthem by Act of Congress in 1931, contains these verses:

> Blest with victory and peace, may the heav'n rescued land
> Praise the Pow'r that hath made and preserved us a nation!
> Then conquer we must, when our cause it is just,
> And this be our motto "In God is our Trust."

In 1954 Congress added a phrase to the Pledge of Allegiance to the Flag so that it now contains the words "one Nation *under God,* indivisible, with liberty and justice for all." In 1952 Congress enacted legislation calling upon the President each year to proclaim a National Day of Prayer. Since 1865 the words "IN GOD WE TRUST" have been impressed on our coins.

Countless similar examples could be listed, but there is no need to belabor the obvious. It was all summed up by this Court just ten years ago in a single sentence: "We are a religious people whose institutions presuppose a Supreme Being." *Zorach v. Clauson,* 343 U.S. 306, 313.

I do not believe that this Court, or the Congress, or the President has by the actions and practices I have mentioned established an "official religion" in violation of the Constitution. And I do not believe the State of New York has done so in this case. What each has done has been to recognize and to follow the deeply entrenched and highly cherished spiritual traditions of our Nation—traditions which come down to us from those who almost two hundred years ago avowed their "firm reliance on the Protection of Divine Providence" when they proclaimed the freedom and independence of this brave new world.

VII

[From the 8–1 majority opinion in the Schempp and Murray cases (1963) wherein the Supreme Court ruled unconstitutional Bible-reading and the recitation of the Lord's Prayer in public schools. In this decision, the Supreme Court summed up its previous findings, quoted heavily from them in substantiating the concept of state "neutrality" in religious affairs and concluded:]

The wholesome "neutrality" of which this Court's cases speak thus stems from a recognition of the teachings of history that powerful sects or groups might bring about a fusion of governmental and religious functions or a concert or dependency of one upon the other to the end that official support of the state or Federal Government would be placed behind the tenets of one or of all orthodoxies. This the establishment clause prohibits.

And a further reason for neutrality is found in the free exercise clause, which recognizes the value of religious training, teaching and observance and, more particularly, the right of every person to freely choose his own course with reference thereto, free of any compulsion from the state. This the free exercise clause guarantees.

Thus, as we have seen, the two clauses may overlap. As we have indicated the establishment clause has been directly considered by this Court eight times in the past

score of years and, with only one Justice dissenting on
the point, it has consistently held that the clause with-
drew all legislative power respecting religious belief or
the expression thereof.

GUIDE RULES SUGGESTED

The test may be stated as follows: What are the purpose and the primary effect of the enactment?

If either is the advancement or inhibition of religion
then the enactment exceeds the scope of legislative power
as circumscribed by the Constitution. That is to say that
to withstand the strictures of the establishment clause
there must be a secular legislative purpose and a primary
effect that neither advances nor inhibits religion.

The free exercise clause, likewise considered many
times here, withdraws from legislative power, State and
Federal, the exertion of any restraint on the free exercise
of religion. Its purpose is to secure religious liberty in the
individual by prohibiting any invasions thereof by civil
authority. Hence it is necessary in a free exercise case for
one to show the coercive effect of the enactment as it
operates against him in the practice of his religion.

The distinction between the two clauses is apparent—
a violation of the free exercise clause is predicated on
coercion while the establishment clause violation need not
be so attended.

Applying the establishment clause principles to the
cases at bar we find that the states are requiring the
selection and reading at the opening of the school day of
verses from the Holy Bible and the recitation of the Lord's
Prayer by the students in unison. These exercises are prescribed as part of the curricular activities of students who
are required by law to attend school. They are held in the
school buildings under the supervision and with the participation of teachers employed in those schools . . .

The conclusion follows that in both cases the laws
require religious exercises and such exercises are being
conducted in direct violation of the rights of the ap-

pellees and petitioners. Nor are these required exercises mitigated by the fact that individual students may absent themselves upon parental request, for that fact furnishes no defense to a claim of unconstitutionality under the establishment clause.

Further, it is no defense to urge that the religious practices here may be relatively minor encroachments on the First Amendment. The breach of neutrality that is today a trickling stream may all too soon become a raging torrent and, in the words of Madison, "It is proper to take alarm at the first experiment on our liberties."

It is insisted that unless these religious exercises are permitted "religion of secularism" is established in the schools. We agree of course, that the state may not establish a "religion of secularism" in the sense of affirmatively opposing or showing hostility to religion, thus "preferring those who believe in no religion over those who do believe." We do not agree, however, that this decision in any sense has that effect.

In addition, it might well be said that one's education is not complete without a study of comparative religion or the history of religion and its relationship to the advancement of civilization. It certainly may be said that the Bible is worthy of study for its literary and historic qualities.

Nothing we have said here indicates that such study of the Bible or of religion, when presented objectively as part of a secular program of education, may not be effected consistent with the First Amendment. But the exercises here do not fall into those categories. They are religious exercises, required by the states in violation of the command of the First Amendment that the government maintain strict neutrality, neither aiding nor opposing religion.

Finally, we cannot accept that the concept of neutrality, which does not permit a state to require a religious exercise even with the consent of the majority of those affected, collides with the majority's right to free exercise of religion.

While the free exercise clause clearly prohibits the

use of state action to deny the right of free exercise to any-one it has never meant that a majority could use the machinery of the state to practice its beliefs. Such a contention was effectively answered by Mr. Justice Jackson for the Court in West Virginia Board of Education v. Barnette.

"The very purpose of a Bill of Rights was to withdraw certain subjects from the vicissitudes of political controversy, to place them beyond the reach of majorities and officials and to establish them as legal principles to be applied by the courts. One's right to . . . freedom of worship . . . and other fundamental rights may not be submitted to vote; they depend on the outcome of no elections."

The place of religion in our society is an exalted one, achieved through a long tradition of reliance on the home, the church and the inviolable citadel of the individual heart and mind. We have come to recognize through bitter experience that it is not within the power of government to invade that citadel, whether its purpose or effect be to aid or oppose, to advance or retard.

In the relationship between man and religion, the state is firmly committed to a position of neutrality. Though the application of that rule requires interpretation of a delicate sort, the rule itself is clearly and concisely stated in the words of the First Amendment.

COMMUNITY CONFLICT:

CHRISTMAS OBSERVANCE IN THE PUBLIC SCHOOLS

THE SETTING

Hamdem, Connecticut, is a prosperous suburban town on the northern border of New Haven. Originally a semi-rural community, Hamden has grown rapidly since World War II, following the pattern of small towns that have developed into residential suburbs of a nearby city. Most of its truck farms have been replaced by moderate or expensive homes that continue the upper-middle-class tradition of the town and by a number of large and cheaper housing developments.

The average family income of its 41,000 residents is among the highest in the state. Like many other affluent suburbs (along with its well-to-do commuting residents, the town has also developed extensive commercial facilities), Hamden has a sizable number of secure, well-informed, independent citizens who take an active interest in community affairs. At the same time, Hamden has been a changing community, and its predominantly upper-middle-class way of life has begun to be altered by the influx of lower-income families in the housing developments.

There has also been an increasing diversity in its ethnic and religious groupings. The religious pattern is now approximately the same as it is in the state as a whole; roughly 50 per cent of its citizens are Catholic and about 10 per cent are Jewish; the rest are either Protestant or unaffiliated with any religious group. Though some observers have reported that a rise in intergroup tension and conflict has accompanied the changes in the social and cultural pattern of the town, nonetheless Hamden has by and large maintained the placid and orderly character of its pre-World War II days.

According to a Hamden Selectman who has lived in the city all his life, the relations among the townspeople have remained friendly, and, in fact, the town has been a model community with respect to the fellowship and understanding among groups that have widely disparate ethnic, religious, intellectual, and social backgrounds. On the whole, then, Hamden was an unlikely setting for the religious strife and bigotry that suddenly broke out there in early December 1961, and the Selectman, among many others, was shocked at the wave of animosity that was produced among its citizens before the controversy died down.

HOW THE CONTROVERSY BEGAN

The public schools of Hamden, like most of those throughout the state, have included Christmas observances in their regular educational program. For example, children in the elementary grades are encouraged to draw nativity scenes, while the older students take part in Christmas pageants and carol singing. Non-Christian children are not required to participate in these observances. During December, the Hamden schools also celebrate the Jewish festival of Hanukkah, with Christian children offered a similar option.

On November 10th, 1961, both types of observances were challenged by the New Haven Jewish Community Council. A letter and an accompanying resolution were sent to the boards of education of the five municipalities in the Greater New Haven area.

The letter, signed by Rabbi Richard Israel, Chairman of the JCC's Community Relations Committee, was addressed to the point that "our society has the obligation to aid its individual members in maintaining their religious integrity." The accompanying resolution declared that the First Amendment to the Constitution "is violated by the practice of introducing prayers or other religious exercises such as the celebration of religious holidays" in the public schools. For this reason the JCC could "give no sanction to Jewish religious observances of any kind in the public schools of our community." While the JCC expressed "deep appreciation" for invitations from school authorities to "share in joint religious exercises, including joint celebrations of sacred holidays," the resolution went on to state that "our concern over basic principles and for the future of religious freedom of all Americans dictates that we should not participate." The JCC also urged Americans of all faiths to "join with us in abjuring any forms of public sponsorship of religious exercises, celebrations and festivals within America's public schools" and to "guard with scrupulous care the wall of separation between church and state erected by the founding fathers of this republic and incorporated in its fundamental law."

The letter and resolution was followed almost two weeks later by a news story on the JCC's request in the New Haven *Register* of November 22, in which Rabbi Israel was quoted as saying, "The holiday season should be a season of goodwill and brotherhood. It is a shame when sectarian celebrations instead promise divisiveness." Throughout most of the New Haven area, there was little apparent attention paid to the JCC's position. However, in Hamden action was being taken—albeit in a slow manner. A memo was drafted by School Superintendent David Wyllie which ordered the Hamden schools to "play down" the religious aspect of their Christmas observances. Holiday decorations with religious motifs were to be eliminated, and no nativity pageants or other religious ceremonies were to be permitted. The new policy did allow Christmas carols and other music of "ecclesiastical origin" to be performed at school assemblies and did not restrict secular observances of the holiday. In effect, the new policy was to "confine observances primarily to holiday aspects." Mr. Wyllie's memo was dated November 15th but did not reach the schools before the beginning of December. The first public word of the order appeared in the New Haven *Journal-Courier* on December 4th. In the news story Wyllie was quoted as saying that his action was prompted by the JCC's resolution and not by any local complaints.

By the time the Wyllie memo was circulated in the schools, the preparations for the customary decorations and pageants were already underway. Some observers believed that the belated timing of the order contributed significantly to the hostile reaction it produced among students and teachers. Others suggested that Wyllie's unpopularity among some in the Hamden community was also an important factor in the controversy that ensued. The wife of an important Hamden official described Wyllie as "a very good business manager but a poor public relations man." She said that Hamden residents had been particularly critical of a school board policy, for which Wyllie was held primarily responsible, of conducting lengthy executive sessions prior to virtually every public meeting, which created the impression that Wyllie and the school board were "trying to keep things from the public." It is worth noting that the manner in which the new policy was handled at a public meeting on the evening following the appearance of the ruling in the press, gives considerable support to this charge. On the other hand, the chairman of the Hamden Board of Education attributed the source of the controversy to inflammatory newspaper coverage of the Wyllie memo.

"There was a lot of misunderstanding," he said. "It was flared up by newspapers and the parents got excited." The chairman's charge against the press was echoed by a number of other informants, who contended that if the story which appeared in the *Journal-Courier* had presented a more "balanced" coverage of the facts, the emotional reaction in the town would not have been so prompt and heated. But whatever the underlying causes for the public reaction, it developed quickly. Along with the extensive coverage in the New Haven and neighboring newspapers, certain opponents of the new policy drummed up community interest and antipathy by initiating chain telephone calls. The controversy was also fanned by rapid developments within the local churches, the community, and within the schools themselves.

FUEL IS ADDED TO THE FIRE

On Monday evening of December 4th, some twelve hours after the first word of the Wyllie order had reached the public, the pastor of St. Rita's Church in Hamden and dean of the New Haven (West) deanery read to his parishioners an editorial from the December issue of *Columbia*. The official monthly magazine of the Knights of Columbus, *Columbia* has its editorial offices in New Haven, and the editorial quoted at length from the JCC's resolution and argued against it, though without specifying that the scene of the issue was New Haven. The editorial began with the statement that "among the vanishing arts is the useful one of leaving well enough alone," and after reviewing the JCC's argument, went on to deplore the danger of "divisiveness" arising from this new disturbance to the "easy, give-and-take atmosphere that prevailed in the community and its schools" over celebrating Christmas and Hanukkah. The editorial wound up by expressing confidence that "the majority, and, surely, the most thoughtful of our Jewish brethren" appreciate the importance of Christmas "to many millions of our people" and do not desire "to diminish its observance—even the circumspect observance that occurs in many, if not most, public schools. The Republic has survived more potent threats than any represented in pinning up some children's drawings of the Mother and Child with attending angels. The danger of having a state-imposed religion fastened upon us does not grow from such seed."

Several informants have said that they were told by responsible observers that the pastor had read the editorial calmly and added no comments of his own. There was, however, considerable distortion of the incident. News of his reading of the editorial spread quickly by word of mouth and the rumors were that he had launched an "intemperate attack" on Wyllie and the Board of Education and that he had exhorted his parishioners to join in attacking the ruling. There is no evidence that either of these rumors was true, but by next morning there were few persons in Hamden who did not know that the ranking clergyman in Hamden had spoken out in some fashion on the Wyllie directive.

The editorial read by the Catholic priest was considerably more moderate than a statement issued on the same day by the minister of a local Protestant church. In a statement given to the press on December 4th, the minister argued that "culturally the United States of America is Christian" and that "when any people become so divisive that they refuse to listen to the prayers and songs and traditions of another's faith then God is becoming a distant reality." The conclusion that the minister reached was that the resolution by the JCC was an "unreasonable request to keep religion out of human life. It is our firm conviction that in Jesus God gave man the greatest revelation of himself—we only show our appreciation when we celebrate His birthday in every phase of our living."

MUNICIPAL REACTIONS: THE OPEN MEETING

As the Hamden community became aware of the new policy, both school and civic officials received a mounting barrage of phone calls and letters. First Selectman DeNicola was quoted in the press as follows: "I have been swamped by calls and letters, and may I say that many of them have been nasty. They have sickened me." By Tuesday evening the reaction in the community was already reaching a climax. The occasion was an open meeting of the Board of Education. Because of the massive attendance at the meeting, its site had to be shifted to a junior high school auditorium and well over 500 townspeople jammed their way in. Gilbert Ames, a New Haven real estate man and a long-time resident of Hamden, offered the following account of the meeting:

"When the meeting started in the auditorium, the school authorities insulted the crowd and made it very angry.

Bing (Bingham) Humphrey commented on the great size of the crowd and then said, 'But regardless, this [the superintendent's directive] will not be discussed tonight.'

"Several persons in the crowd yelled insults at Humphrey and were demanding that he not tell us what to do.

"Humphrey did not recognize any speakers. People got up and yelled and the person who yelled loudest spoke. Humphrey said the Board of Education was going into this cold and didn't have all the facts. Humphrey said Wyllie had spoken to him before issuing the directive and he (Humphrey) left it up to him.

"After five or ten minutes of this complete disorder, I got up and suggested a very simple way to handle this. I suggested the Board take a vote then and there whether to back Wyllie's directive or not. 'Each Board member should vote in open session,' I said.

"One member of the Board stood up—I forget who—and said he didn't think the Board should have to vote in the open. A second member stood up and agreed. The Board left the room to go into executive session and left Wyllie and his assistant, William Schleicher, alone on the stage to face the crowd.

"Wyllie started to read his directive to the crowd. When he was almost finished, the Board called him into the executive session, leaving Schleicher alone.

"Before leaving, Wyllie requested Schleicher to continue the reading of the directive and also the letter from the Jewish Community Council.

"This is when the trouble really started. Schleicher said he would read the letter from the Jewish Council but didn't see why he should. 'We have wasted enough time with you people already. I don't think you're worth it,' he said.

"While I was talking to Schleicher trying to get him to apologize, two men rushed by me and also demanded he apologize. While we were talking, two police detectives and a police sergeant came to the front of the room and separated all concerned. There was absolutely no violence at any time.

"The crowd was very angry; angry at the school authorities and at the Jewish people and leaders.

"One man got up to speak and said he was a Jew.

"Someone jumped to his feet and yelled, 'Go home; we don't want your kind here!'

"Another person yelled, 'Give him a chance to talk! Let's hear what he has to say!'

"The person said he was not in favor of the request of the Jewish Council.

"There were about 650 to 700 persons there. Maybe 50 were directly involved in the discussions and were angry enough to yell and shout. Most of the rest were behind them and applauded each speaker."

Ames gave the impression that he felt that supporters of the Wyllie directive would have been very reluctant to stand up and speak before the crowd, considering its mood. Ames' comments on the episode appeared to be typical of the views of a great many of his townsmen:

"Too many people want to change our American way of life. I can't see change for change's sake and I don't think they should try to jam these things down the people's throats."

One of Hamden's most respected citizens believes that it is fair to compare the meeting, to a mob in Munich under Hitler or a White Citizens Council meeting in Atlanta.

Another informant, who also attended the meeting, reports that at one point an elderly man sitting two rows in front of Philip Bear turned around and shouted to him, "I can tell by the nose on your face that you're a Communist kike." The informant estimates, however, that less than 10 per cent of the audience were noisy and disrespectful. "In any community," he said, "you get people who are narrow-minded and ignorant. Some of them showed up and made trouble at the meeting."

After a number of policemen had prevented the meeting from becoming violent over Schleicher's statement to the audience, there were some further speakers. First Selectman DeNicola deplored the "bitter protests" that had been made, while Third Selectman William Adams argued that the reaction represented a "display of faith" and not of prejudice. A member of the Hamden Post of the Jewish War Veterans said that the vast majority of the Jewish population did not support the JCC's resolution and action and that the resolution had been "merely a statement to be considered"—not one that anticipated "immediate and arbitrary action."

After more than an hour, the Board of Education returned from its executive session and announced that Wyllie's directive had been rescinded.

The "lack of Christian charity" displayed at the open meeting was deplored in a joint statement by Protestant clergymen of Hamden. Another minister, Richard E. Smeltzer of the Hamden Plains Methodist Church, commented as follows in his church bulletin:

"About 500 people were present, and most were out for blood. I wish I could communicate to you the abusiveness and violence in the air that night among the 'Christian' majority . . . It was the mood of the western movie just before someone produces the rope, saying, 'We can handle this ourselves, boys—let's not wait for the sheriff.' This is no exaggeration. You just wouldn't have believed that it could happen in Hamden."

THE SEVERITY OF THE REACTION

A spokesman of the Anti-Defamation League, with offices in New Haven, conducted an intensive investigation of events that occurred while controversy raged in Hamden. He reported the following:

1. Postcards were sent to several Jewish merchants in downtown New Haven stating that they would be boycotted because of the Hamden incident. The ADL executive himself saw three or four of the cards. He said the cards "implied" that they were the handiwork of "an organized group with many members."

2. Hamden Jewish merchants were told by "some" peo-

ple that they would be boycotted but, to the investigator's knowledge, they received no threatening postcards.

3. Swastikas were painted on the exterior and interior of the high school. The ADL executive interviewed one student who said he saw the swastikas being washed off.

4. Placards equating "Jews and Communists" were displayed briefly at the high school. They were destroyed almost immediately by school officials.

5. The ADL official has "reason to believe" that notes of a menacing nature were placed in the lockers of Jewish students, though he was unable to substantiate this charge.

It was also reported that Jewish students had been forced to sing Christmas carols, but there was found no evidence to bear this out. The most shocking incident that was rumored to have occurred during the week in Hamden was a series of signs on the blackboards of the Hamden High School, such as "What Eichmann started, we'll finish."

The ranking Catholic prelate, following the school board meeting, instructed all Catholic priests in Hamden to appeal for mutual understanding from their pulpits. The prelate also released a statement to the press. By Sunday, the incidents of the past week were being widely deplored in the churches of Hamden, and the controversy itself appeared to have died down as quickly as it had arisen.

However, the Hamden *Chronicle* of December 7, 1961, described the town as "shattered as never before in its history." And though the outward signs of intergroup hostility have disappeared, an undertone of resentment and bigotry remains. There have been insinuations that a Hamden rabbi was associated with subversive organizations. As Charles P. Lenehan, publisher of the Hamden *Chronicle*, remarked, "There are groups beyond Hamden who for their own purposes want to keep the issue alive." Gilbert Ames, who was the most outspoken critic of the Wyllie policy at the open meeting, reported that he has since received "dozens" of "right-wing" and anti-Semitic publications through the mail.

CRITIQUE

The Chairman of the Hamden Board of Education reported that the following lesson had been learned:

"We have learned one lesson from this," the chairman said. "We will do something that several other communities have done. We will set up an advisory committee (to the school board) consisting of clergymen. In the future, anything like this will be referred to the committee and the board will act on their recommendation. I would imagine we would go along with their recommendation 99 per cent of the time."

The lesson of the open meeting of December 5th, and of the week in Hamden as a whole, was stated by the Rev. Richard E. Smeltzer in a bulletin to the members of the Hamden Plains Methodist Church—all but two of whom had stayed away from the meeting:

"The immediate question raised in the light of Tuesday evening is the degree of real social concern among church people.

"When church people stay away in droves from controversial public meetings and thereby fail to exercise the moderating forces of intelligence and charity, it is not surprising if a belligerent and emotional mob takes over.

"This is a lesson which we must begin to learn if we are to maintain a responsible relationship to the community in which we live."

AMERICA'S FOUR CONSPIRACIES

John Courtney Murray

I

The "free society" seems to be a phrase of American coinage. At least it has no comparable currency in any other language, ancient or modern. The same is true of the phrase "free government." This fact of itself suggests the assumption that American society and its form of government are a unique historical realization. The assumption is generally regarded among us as unquestionable.

However, we have tended of late to pronounce the phrase, "the free society," with a rising interrogatory inflection. The phrase itself, it seems, now formulates a problem. This is an interesting new development. It was once assumed that the American proposition, both social and political, was self-evident; that it authenticated itself on simple inspection; that it was, in consequence, intuitively grasped and generally understood by the American people. This assumption now stands under severe question.

What is the free society, in its "idea"? Is this "idea" being successfully realized in the institutions that presently determine the pattern of American life, social and personal? The web of American institutions has altered, rapidly and profoundly, even radically, over the past few generations. Has the "idea" of the free society perhaps been strangled by the tightening intricacies of the newly formed institutional network? Has some new and alien "idea" subtly and unsuspectedly assumed the role of an organizing force in American society? Do we understand not only the superficial facts of change in American life but also the underlying factors of change—those "variable constants" that forever provide the dynamisms of change in all human life?

The very fact that these questions are being asked makes it sharply urgent that they be answered. What is at stake is America's understanding of itself. Self-understanding is the necessary condition of a sense of self-identity and self-confidence, whether in the case of an individual or in the case of a people. If the American people can no longer base this sense on naïve assumptions of self-evidence, it is imperative that they find other more reasoned grounds for their essential affirmation that they are uniquely a people, uniquely a free society. Otherwise the peril is great. The complete loss of one's identity is, with all propriety of theological definition, hell. In diminished forms it is insanity. And it would not be well for the American giant to go lumbering about the world today, lost and mad.

At this juncture I suggest that the immediate question is not whether the free society is really free. This question may be unanswerable; it may even be meaningless as a question, if only for the reason that the norms of freedom seem to have got lost in a welter of confused controversy. Therefore I suggest that the immediate question is whether American society is properly civil. This question is intelligible and answerable, because the basic standard of civility is not in doubt: "Civilization is formed by men locked together in argument. From this dialogue the community becomes a political community."[1] This statement exactly expresses the mind of St. Thomas Aquinas, who was himself giving refined expression to the tradition of classic antiquity, which in its prior turn had given first elaboration to the concept of the "civil multitude," the multitude that is not a mass or a herd or a huddle, because it is characterized by civility.

The specifying note of political association is its rational deliberative quality, its dependence for its permanent cohesiveness on argument among men. In this it differs

[1] Thomas Gilby, O.P., *Between Community and Society* (London: Longmans Green, 1953), p. 93.

from all other forms of association found on earth. The animal kingdom is held together simply by the material homogeneity of the species; all its unities and antagonisms are of the organic and biological order. Wolves do not argue the merits of running in packs. The primal human community, the family, has its own distinctive bonds of union. Husband and wife are not drawn into the marital association simply by the forces of reason but by the forces of life itself, importantly including the mysterious dynamisms of sex. Their association is indeed founded on a contract, which must be a rational and free act. But the substance and finality of the contract is both infra- and supra-rational; it is an engagement to become "two in one flesh." The marital relationship may at times be quarrelsome, but it is not argumentative. Similarly, the union of parents and children is not based on reason, justice, or power; it is based on kinship, love, and *pietas*.

It is otherwise with the political community. I am not, of course, maintaining that civil society is a purely rational form of association. We no longer believe, with Locke or Hobbes, that man escapes from a mythical "state of nature" by an act of will, by a social contract. Civil society is a need of human nature before it becomes the object of human choice. Moreover, every particular society is a creature of the soil; it springs from the physical soil of earth and from the more formative soil of history. Its existence is sustained by loyalties that are not logical; its ideals are expressed in legends that go beyond the facts and are for that reason vehicles of truth; its cohesiveness depends in no small part on the materialisms of property and interest. Though all this is true, nevertheless the distinctive bond of the civil multitude is reason, or more exactly, that exercise of reason which is argument.

Hence the climate of the City is likewise distinctive. It is not feral or familial but forensic. It is not hot and humid, like the climate of the animal kingdom. It lacks the cordial warmth of love and unreasoning loyalty that pervades the family. It is cool and dry, with the coolness and dryness that characterize good argument among informed and responsible men. Civic amity gives to this climate its vital quality. This form of friendship is a special kind of moral virtue, a thing of reason and intelligence, laboriously cultivated by the discipline of passion, prejudice, and narrow self-interest. It is the sentiment proper to the City. It has nothing to do with the cleavage of a David to a Jonathan, or with the kinship of the clan, or with the charity, *fortis ut mors,* that makes the solidarity of the Church. It is in direct contrast with the passionate fanaticism of the Jacobin: "Be my brother or I'll kill you!" Ideally, I suppose, there should be only one passion in the City—the passion for justice. But the will to justice, though it engages the heart, finds its measure as it finds its origin in intelligence, in a clear understanding of what is due to the equal citizen from the City and to the City from the citizenry according to the mode of their equality. This commonly shared will to justice is the ground of civic amity as it is also the ground of that unity which is called peace. This unity, qualified by amity, is the highest good of the civil multitude and the perfection of its civility.

If, then, society is civil when it is formed by men locked together in argument, the question rises, what is the argument about? There are three major themes.

First, the argument is about public affairs, the *res publica,* those matters which are for the advantage of the public (in the phrase as old as Plato) and which call for public decision and action by government. These affairs have their origin in matters of fact; but their rational discussion calls for the Socratic dialogue, the close and easy use of the habit of cross-examination, that transforms brute facts into arguable issues.

Second, the public argument concerns the affairs of the commonwealth. This is a wider concept. It denotes the affairs that fall, at least in decisive part, beyond the limited scope of government. These affairs are not to be settled by law, though law may be in some degree relevant to their settlement. They go beyond the necessities of the public order as such; they bear upon the quality of the common life. The great "affair" of the commonwealth is, of course, education. It includes three general areas of common interest: the school system, its mode of organization, its curricular content, and the level of learning among its teachers; the later education of the citizen in the liberal art of citizenship; and the more general enterprise of the advancement of knowledge by research.

The third theme of public argument is the most important and the most difficult. It concerns the constitutional consensus whereby the people acquires its identity as a people and the society is endowed with its vital form, its entelechy, its sense of purpose as a collectivity organized for action in history. The idea of consensus has been classic since the Stoics and Cicero; through St. Augustine it found its way into the liberal tradition of the West: *"Res publica, res populi; populus autem non omnis hominum coetus quoquo modo congregatus, sed coetus multitudinis iuris consensu et utilitatis communione sociatus"* (Scipio).

The state of civility supposes a consensus that is constitutional, *sc.*, its focus is the idea of law, as surrounded by the whole constellation of ideas that are related to the *ratio iuris* as its premises, its constituent elements, and its consequences. This consensus is come to by the people; they become a people by coming to it. They do not come to it accidentally, without quite knowing how, but deliberatively, by the methods of reason reflecting on experience. The consensus is not a structure of secondary rationalizations erected on psychological data (as the behaviorist would have it) or on economic data (as the Marxist would have it). It is not the residual minimum left after rigid application of the Cartesian axiom, *"de omnibus dubitandum."* It is not simply a set of working hypotheses whose value is pragmatic. It is an ensemble of substantive truths, a structure of basic knowledge, an order of elementary affirmations that reflect realities inherent in the order of existence. It occupies an established position in society and excludes opinions alien or contrary to itself. This consensus is the intuitional *a priori* of all the rationalities and technicalities of constitutional and statutory law. It furnishes the premises of the people's action in history and defines the larger aims which that action seeks in internal affairs and in external relations.

It is to this idea of consensus, I take it, that the Declaration of Independence adverts: "We hold these truths to be self-evident. . . ." I know, of course, that a good bit of sophisticated fun has been poked at this eighteenth-century sentence. But when the sophisticated gentry has had its fun, the essential meaning of the sentence remains intact and its political significance stands unimpaired. The original American affirmation was simply this: "There are truths, and we hold them as the foundations of our political existence as a constitutional commonwealth."

This consensus is the ultimate theme of the public argument whereby American society hopes to achieve and maintain the mark of civility. The whole premise of the argument, if it is to be civilized and civilizing, is that the consensus is real, that among the people everything is not in doubt, but that there is a core of agreement, accord, concurrence, acquiescence. We hold certain truths; therefore we can argue about them. It seems to have been one of the corruptions of intelligence by positivism to assume that argument ends when agreement is reached. In a basic sense the reverse is true. There can be no argument except on the premise, and within a context, of agreement. *Mutatis mutandis*, this is true of scientific, philosophical, and theological argument. It is no less true of political argument.

On its most imperative level the public argument within the City and about the City's affairs begins with the agreement that there is a reality called, in the phrase of Leo XIII, *patrimonium generis humani*, a heritage of an essential truth, a tradition of rational belief, that sustains the structure of the City and furnishes the substance of civil life. It was to this patrimony that the Declaration of Independence referred: "These are the truths we hold." This is the first utterance of a people. By it a people establishes its identity, and under decent respect to the opinions of mankind declares its purposes within the community of nations.

II

The truths we hold were well enough stated. Three are immediate: the limitation of government by law—by a higher law not of government's making, whereby an order of inviolable rights is constituted; the principle of consent; and the right of resistance to unjust rule. These are the heritage of classical and medieval constitutionalism; they center on the idea of law. One truth is remote and meta-political—that man is not the creature of the City but of God; that the dignity of man is equal in all men; that there are human purposes which transcend the order of politics; that the ultimate function of the political order is to support man in the pursuit of these purposes; that it is within the power of man to alter his own history in pursuit of his own good. You will not find this pregnant truth elsewhere than in the Western and Christian heritage.

Initially, we hold these truths because they are a patri-mony. They are a heritage from history, through whose dark and bloody pages there runs like a silver thread the tradition of civility. This is the first reason why the con-sensus continually calls for public argument. The consensus is an intellectual heritage; it may be lost to mind or de-formed in the mind. Its final depository is the public mind. This is indeed a perilous place to deposit what ought to be kept safe; for the public mind is exposed to the corrosive rust of skepticism, to the predatory moths of deceitful doxai (in Plato's sense), and to the incessant thieveries of forgetfulness. Therefore the consensus can only be pre-served in the public mind by argument. High argument alone will keep it alive, in the vital state of being "held."

Second, we hold these truths because they are true. They have been found in the structure of reality by that dialectic of observation and reflection which is called philosophy. But as the achievement of reason and experience the consensus again presents itself for argument. Its vitality depends on a constant scrutiny of political experience, as this experience widens with the developing—or possibly the decaying—life of man in society. Only at the price of this continued contact with experience will a constitutional tradition continue to be "held," as real knowledge and not simply as a structure of prejudice. However, the tradition, or the consensus, is not a mere record of experience. It is experience illumined by principle, given a construction by a process of philosophical reflection. In the public argument there must consequently be a continued recurrence to first principles. Otherwise the consensus may come to seem simply a projection of ephemeral experience, a passing shadow on the vanishing backdrop of some given historical scene, without the permanence proper to truths that are "held."

On both of these titles, as a heritage and as a public philosophy, the American consensus needs to be constantly argued. If the public argument dies from disinterest, or subsides into the angry mutterings of polemic, or rises to the shrillness of hysteria, or trails off into positivistic triviality, or gets lost in a morass of semantics, you may be sure that the barbarian is at the gates of the City.

The barbarian need not appear in bearskins with a club in hand. He may wear a Brooks Brothers suit and carry a ball-point pen with which to write his advertising copy. In fact, even beneath the academic gown there may lurk a child of the wilderness, untutored in the high tradition of civility, who goes busily and happily about his work, a domesticated and law-abiding man, engaged in the construction of a philosophy to put an end to all philosophy, and thus put an end to the possibility of a vital consensus and to civility itself. This is perennially the work of the barbarian, to undermine rational standards of judgment, to corrupt the inherited intuitive wisdom by which the people have always lived, and to do this not by spreading new beliefs but by creating a climate of doubt and bewilderment in which clarity about the larger aims of life is dimmed and the self-confidence of the people is destroyed, so that finally what you have is the impotent nihilism of the "generation of the third eye," now presently appearing on our university campuses. (One is, I take it, on the brink of impotence and nihilism when one begins to be aware of one's own awareness of what one is doing, saying, thinking. This is the paralysis of all serious thought; it is likewise the destruction of all the spontaneities of love.)

The barbarian may be the eighteenth-century philosopher, who neither anticipated nor desired the brutalities of the Revolution with its Committee on the Public Safety, but who prepared the ways for the Revolution by creating a vacuum which he was not able to fill. Today the barbarian is the man who makes open and explicit the rejection of the traditional role of reason and logic in human affairs. He is the man who reduces all spiritual and moral questions to the test of practical results or to an analysis of language or to decision in terms of individual subjective feeling.

It is a Christian theological intuition, confirmed by all of historical experience, that man lives both his personal and his social life always more or less close to the brink of barbarism, threatened not only by the disintegrations of physical illness and by the disorganizations of mental imbalance, but also by the decadence of moral corruption and the political chaos of formlessness or the moral chaos of tyranny. Society is rescued from chaos only by a few men, not by the many. *Paucis humanum vivit genus.* It is only the few who understand the disciplines of civility and are able to sustain them in being and thus hold in check the forces of barbarism that are always threatening to force the gates of the City. To say this is not, of course, to endorse the concept of the fascist élite—a barbarous concept, if ever there was one. It is only to recall a lesson of history to which our own era of mass civilization may well attend. We have not been behind our forebears in devising both gross and subtle ways of massacring ancient civilities.

Barbarism is not, I repeat, the forest primeval with all its relatively simple savageries. Barbarism has long had its definition, resumed by St. Thomas after Aristotle. It is the lack of reasonable conversation according to reasonable laws. Here the word "conversation" has its twofold Latin sense. It means living together and talking together.

Barbarism threatens when men cease to live together according to reason, embodied in law and custom, and incorporated in a web of institutions that sufficiently reveal rational influences, even though they are not, and cannot be, wholly rational. Society becomes barbarian when men are huddled together under the rule of force and fear; when economic interests assume the primacy over higher values; when material standards of mass and quantity crush out the values of quality and excellence; when technology assumes an autonomous existence and embarks on a course of unlimited self-exploitation without purposeful guidance from the higher disciplines of politics and morals; when the state reaches the paradoxical point of being everywhere intrusive and also impotent, possessed of immense power and powerless to achieve rational ends; when the ways of men come under the sway of the instinctual, the impulsive, the compulsive. When things like this happen, barbarism is abroad, whatever the surface impressions of urbanity. Men have ceased to live together according to reasonable laws.

Barbarism likewise threatens when men cease to talk together according to reasonable laws. There are laws of argument, the observance of which is imperative if discourse is to be civilized. Argument ceases to be civil when it is dominated by passion and prejudice; when its vocabulary becomes solipsist, premised on the theory that my insight is mine alone and cannot be shared; when dialogue gives way to a series of monologues; when the parties to the conversation cease to listen to one another, or hear only what they want to hear, or see the other's argument only through the screen of their own categories; when defiance is flung to the basic ontological principle of all ordered discourse, which asserts that Reality is an analogical structure, within which there are variant modes of reality, to each of which there corresponds a distinctive method of thought that imposes on argument its own special rules. When things like this happen men cannot be locked together in argument. Conversation becomes merely quarrelsome or querulous. Civility dies with the death of the dialogue.

All this has been said in order to give some meaning to the immediate question before us, *sc.*, whether American society, which calls itself free, is genuinely civil. In any circumstances it has always been difficult to achieve civility in the sense explained. A group of men locked together in argument is a rare spectacle. But within the great sprawling City that is the United States the achievement of a civil society encounters a special difficulty—what is called religious pluralism.

III

The political order must borrow both from above itself and from below itself. The political looks upward to metaphysics, ethics, theology; it looks downward to history, legal science, sociology, psychology. The order of politics must reckon with all that is true and factual about man. The problem was complicated enough for Aristotle, for whom man in the end was only citizen, whose final destiny was to be achieved within the City, however much he might long to play the immortal. For us today man is still citizen; but at least for most of us his life is not absorbed in the City, in society and the state. In the citizen who is also a Christian there resides the consciousness formulated immortally in the second-century *Letter to Diognetes:* "Every foreign land is a fatherland and every fatherland is a foreign land." This consciousness makes a difference, in ways upon which we need not dwell here. What makes the more important difference is the fact of religious divisions. Civil discourse would be hard enough if among us there prevailed conditions of religious unity; even in such conditions civic unity would be a complicated and laborious achievement. As it is, efforts at civil discourse plunge us into the twofold experience of the religiously pluralist society.

The first experience is intellectual. As we discourse on public affairs, on the affairs of the commonwealth, and particularly on the problem of consensus, we inevitably have to move upward, as it were, into realms of some theoretical generality—into metaphysics, ethics, theology. This movement does not carry us into disagreement; for disagreement is not an easy thing to reach. Rather, we move into confusion. Among us there is a plurality of universes of discourse. These universes are incommensurable. And when they clash, the issue of agreement or disagreement tends to become irrelevant. The immediate situation is simply one of confusion. One does not know what the other is talking about. One may distrust what the other is driving at. For this too is part of the problem —the disposition amid the confusion to disregard the immediate argument, as made, and to suspect its tendency, to wonder what the man who makes it is really driving at.

This is the pluralist society as it is encountered on the level of intellectual experience. We have no common universe of discourse. In particular, diverse mental equivalents attach to all the words in which the constitutional consensus must finally be discussed—truth, freedom, justice, prudence, order, law, authority, power, knowledge, certainty, unity, peace, virtue, morality, religion, God, and perhaps even man. Our intellectual experience is one of sheer confusion, in which soliloquy succeeds to argument.

The second experience is even more profound. The themes touched upon in any discussion of Religion and the Free Society have all had a long history. And in the course of discussing them we are again made aware that only in a limited sense have we severally had the same history. We more or less share the short segment of history known as America. But all of us have had longer histories, spiritual and intellectual.

These histories may indeed touch at certain points. But I, for instance, am conscious that I do not share the histories that lie behind many of my fellow citizens. The Jew does not share the Christian history, nor even the Christian idea of history. Catholic and Protestant history may be parallel in a limited sense but they are not coincident or coeval. And the secularist is a latecomer. He may locate his ancestry in the eighteenth or nineteenth centuries, or, if his historic sense is strong, he may go back to the fourteenth century, to the rise of what Lagarde has called *l'esprit laïque.* In any case, he cannot go back to Athens, Rome, or Alexandria; for his laicism is historically conditioned. It must situate itself with regard to the Christian tradition. It must include denials and disassociations that the secularism of antiquity did not have to make; and it also includes the affirmation of certain Christian values that antiquity could not have affirmed.

The fact of our discrepant histories creates the second experience of the pluralist society. We are aware that we not only hold different views but have become different kinds of men as we have lived our several histories. Our styles of thought and of interior life are as discrepant as our histories. The more deeply they are experienced and the more fully they are measured, the more do the differences among us appear to be almost unbridgeable. Man is not only a creature of thought but also a vibrant subject of sympathies; and in the realm of philosophy and religion today the communal experiences are so divergent that they create not sympathies but alienations as between groups.

Take, for instance, the question of natural law. For the Catholic it is simply a problem in metaphysical, ethical, and juridical argument; he moves into the argument naturally and feels easy amid its complexities. For the Protestant, on the contrary, the very concept is a challenge, if not an affront, to his whole religiosity, to which it is largely alien and very largely unassimilable.

Another example might be the argument that has been made by Catholics in this country for more than a century with regard to the distribution of tax funds for the support of the school system. The structure of the argument is not complex. Its principle is that the canons of distributive justice ought to control the action of government in allocating funds that it coercively collects from all the people in pursuance of its legitimate interest in universal compulsory schooling. The fact is that these canons are presently not being observed. The "solution" to the School Question reached in the nineteenth century reveals injustice, and the legal statutes that establish the injustice are an abuse of power. So, in drastic brevity, runs the argument. For my part, I have never heard a satisfactory answer to it.

This is a fairly serious situation. When a large section of the community asserts that injustice is being done, and makes a reasonable argument to substantiate the assertion, either the argument ought to be convincingly refuted and the claim of injustice thus disposed of, or the validity of the argument ought to be admitted and the injustice remedied. As a matter of fact, however, the argument customarily meets a blank stare, or else it is "answered" by varieties of the fallacy known as *ignoratio elenchi*. At the extreme, from the side of the more careerist type of anti-Catholic, the rejoinder takes this form, roughly speaking (sometimes the rejoinder is roughly spoken): "We might be willing to listen to this argument about the rights of Catholic schools if we believed that Catholic schools had any rights at all. But we do not grant that they have any rights, except to tolerance. Their existence is not for the advantage of the public; they offend against the integrity of the democratic community, whose warrant is fidelity to Protestant principle (or secularist principle, as the case may be)." This "answer" takes various forms, more or less uncomplimentary to the Catholic Church, according to the temper of the speaker. But this is the gist of it. The statement brings me to my next point.

The fact is that among us civility—or civic unity or civic amity, as you will—is a thing of the surface. It is quite easy to break through it. And when you do, you catch a glimpse of the factual reality of the pluralist society. I agree with Professor Eric Voegelin's thesis that our pluralist society has received its structure through wars and that the wars are still going on beneath a fragile surface of more or less forced urbanity. What Voegelin calls the "genteel picture" will not stand the test of confrontation with fact.

We are not really a group of men singly engaged in the search for truth, relying solely on the means of persuasion, entering into dignified communication with each other, content politely to correct opinions with which we do not agree. As a matter of fact, the variant ideas and allegiances among us are entrenched as social powers; they occupy ground; they have developed interests; and they possess the means to fight for them. The real issues of truth that arise are complicated by secondary issues of power and prestige, which not seldom become primary. Witness, for instance, Catholic defense of the Connecticut birth-rate control statute.[2] It was passed in 1879, in the Comstock era, under Protestant pressure. Its text reveals a characteristic Comstockian ignorance of the rules of tradition jurisprudence; in general, the "free churches" have never understood law but only power, either in the form of majority rule or in the form of minority protest. Since it makes a public crime out of a private sin, and confuses morality with legality, and is unenforceable without police invasion of the bedroom, the statute is indefensible as a law. But the configuration of social power has become such that Catholics now defend it—with a saving sense of irony, I hope.

There are many other examples. What they illustrate is that all the entrenched segments of American pluralism claim influence on the course of events, on the content of the legal order, and on the quality of American society. To each group, of course, its influence seems salvific; to other groups it may seem merely imperialist. In any case, the forces at work are not simply intellectual; they are also passionate. There is not simply an exchange of arguments but of verbal blows. You do not have to probe

[2] The Connecticut Statute was originally Chapter 78, Public Acts of Connecticut, 1879; it is now Section 8568 of the General Statutes, Revision of 1949. It reads as follows: *"Use of drugs or instruments to prevent conception.* Any person who shall use any drug, medicinal article or instrument for the purpose of preventing conception shall be fined not less than fifty dollars or imprisoned not less than sixty days nor more than one year or be both fined and imprisoned." Two decisions have been handed down by the Connecticut Supreme Court of Errors (State *v.* Nelson, 126 Conn. 412 [1940]; and Tileston *v.* Ullman, 129 Conn. 84 [1942]). Both actions were brought, not under the statute itself, but under the general accessory statute (Section 8875, Revision of 1949). Both decisions carried by a vote of three to two.

deeply beneath the surface of civic amity to uncover the structure of passion and war.

There is the ancient resentment of the Jew, who has for centuries been dependent for his existence on the good will, often not forthcoming, of a Christian community. Now in America, where he has acquired social power, his distrust of the Christian community leads him to align himself with the secularizing forces whose dominance, he thinks, will afford him a security he has never known. Again, there is the profound distrust between Catholic and Protestant. Their respective conceptions of Christianity are only analogous; that is, they are partly the same and totally different. The result is *odium theologicum*, a sentiment that not only enhances religious differences in the realm of truth but also creates personal estrangements in the order of charity.

More than that, Catholic and Protestant distrust each other's political intentions. There is the memory of historic clashes in the temporal order; the Irishman does not forget Cromwell any more readily than the Calvinist forgets Louis XIV. Neither Protestant nor Catholic is yet satisfied that the two of them can exist freely and peacefully in the same kind of City. The Catholic regards Protestantism not only as a heresy in the order of religion but also as a corrosive solvent in the order of civilization, whose intentions lead to chaos. The Protestant regards Catholicism not only as idolatry in the order of religion but as an instrument of tyranny in the order of civilization, whose intentions lead to clericalism. Thus an *odium civile* accrues to the *odium theologicum*.

This problem is particularly acute in the United States, where the Protestant was the native and the Catholic the immigrant, in contrast to Europe where the Catholic first held the ground and was only later challenged. If one is to believe certain socio-religious critics Protestantism in America has forged an identification of itself, both historical and ideological, with American culture, particularly with an indigenous secularist unclarified mystique of individual freedom as somehow the source of everything, including justice, order, and unity. The result has been

Nativism in all its manifold forms, ugly and refined, popular and academic, fanatic and liberal. The neo-Nativist as well as the paleo-Nativist addresses to the Catholic substantially the same charge: "You are among us but you are not of us." (The neo-Nativist differs only in that he uses footnotes, apparently in the belief that reference to documents is a substitute for an understanding of them.) To this charge the Catholic, if he happens to set store, *pro forma*, on meriting the blessed adjective "sophisticated," will politely reply that this is Jacobinism, *nouveau style*, and that Jacobinism, any style, is out of style in this day and age. In contrast, the sturdy Catholic War Veteran is more likely to say rudely, "Them's fightin' words." And with this exchange of civilities, if they are such, the "argument" is usually over.

There is, finally, the secularist (I here use the term only in a descriptive sense). He too is at war. If he knows his own history, he must be. Historically his first chosen enemy was the Catholic Church, and it must still be the Enemy of his choice, for two reasons. First, it asserts that there is an authority superior to the authority of individual reason and of the political projection of individual reason, the state. But this assertion is the first object of the secularist's anathema. Second, it asserts that by divine ordinance this world is to be ruled by a dyarchy of authorities, within which the temporal is subordinate to the spiritual, not instrumentally but in dignity. This assertion is doubly anathema. It clashes with the socio-juridical monism that is always basic to the secularist position when it is consistently argued. In secularist theory there can be only one society, one law, one power, and one faith, a civic faith that is the "unifying" bond of the community, whereby it withstands the assaults of assorted pluralisms.

The secularist has always fought his battles under a banner on which is emblazoned his special device, "The Integrity of the Political Order." In the name of this thundering principle he would banish from the political order (and from education as an affair of the City) all the "divisive forces" of religion. At least in America he has traditionally had no quarrel with religion as a "purely private matter," as a sort of essence or idea or ambient aura that may help to warm the hidden heart of solitary man. He may even concede a place to religion-in-general, whatever that is. What alarms him is religion as a Thing, visible, corporate, organized, a community of thought that presumes to sit superior to, and in judgment on, the "community of democratic thought," and that is furnished somehow with an armature of power to make its thought and judgment publicly prevail. Under this threat he marshals his military vocabulary and speaks in terms of aggression, encroachment, maneuvers, strategy, tactics. He rallies to the defense of the City; he sets about the strengthening of the wall that separates the City from its Enemy. He too is at war.

IV

What it comes to then is that the pluralist society, honestly viewed under abdication of all false gentility, is a pattern of interacting conspiracies. There are chiefly four—Protestant, Catholic, Jewish, secularist, though in each camp, to continue the military metaphor, there are forces not fully broken to the authority of the high command.

I would like to relieve the word "conspiracy" of its invidious connotations. It is devoid of these in its original Latin sense, both literal and topical. Literally it means unison, concord, unanimity in opinion and feeling, a "breathing together." Then it acquires inevitably the connotation of united action for a common end about which there is agreement; those who think alike inevitably join together in some manner of action to make their common thought or purpose prevail. The word was part of the Stoic political vocabulary; it was adopted by Cicero; and it has passed into my own philosophical tradition, the Scholastic tradition, that has been formative of the liberal tradition of the West. Civil society is formed, said Cicero, "*conspiratione hominum atque consensu,*" that is by action in concert on the basis of consensus with regard to the purposes of the action. Civil society is by definition a conspiracy, *"conspiratio plurium in unum."* Only by conspiring together do the many become one. *E pluribus unum.*

The trouble is that there are a number of conspiracies within American society. I shall not object to your calling Catholicism a conspiracy, provided you admit that it is only one of several.

Perhaps then our problem today is somehow to make the four great conspiracies among us conspire into one conspiracy that will be American society—civil, just, free, peaceful, one.

Can this problem be solved? My own expectations are modest and minimal. It seems to be the lesson of history that men are usually governed with little wisdom. The highest political good, the unity which is called peace, is far more a goal than a realization. And the search for religious unity, the highest spiritual good, always encounters the "messianic necessity," so-called: "Do you think that I have come to bring peace on earth? No, but rather dissension *(diamerismon)"* (Luke 12:51). In the same text the dissension was predicted with terrible explicitness of the family. It has been the constant lot of the family of nations and of the nations themselves. Religious pluralism is against the will of God. But it is the human condition; it is written into the script of history. It will not somehow marvelously cease to trouble the City.

Advisedly, therefore, one will cherish only modest expectations with regard to the solution of the problem of religious pluralism and civic unity. Utopianism is a Christian heresy (the ancient pagan looked backward, not forward, to the Golden Age); but it is a heresy nonetheless. We cannot hope to make American society the perfect conspiracy based on a unanimous consensus. But we could at least do two things. We could limit the warfare, and we could enlarge the dialogue. We could lay down our arms (at least the more barbarous kind of arms!), and we could take up argument.

Even to do this would not be easy. It would be necessary that we cease to project into the future of the Republic the nightmares, real or fancied, of the past. In

Victorian England, John Henry Newman noted that the Protestant bore "a stain upon the imagination," left there by the vivid images of Reformation polemic against the Church of Rome. Perhaps we all bear some stain or other upon our imaginations. It might be possible to cleanse them by a work of reason. The free society, I said at the outset, is a unique realization; it has inaugurated a new history. Therefore it might be possible within this new history to lay the ghosts of the past—to forget the ghettos and the autos-da-fé; the Star Chamber and the Committee on the Public Safety; Topcliffe with his "Bloody Question" and Torquemada with his rack; the dragonnades and the Black and Tans; Samuel F. B. Morse, the convents in Charleston and Philadelphia, the Know-Nothings and the Ku Klux Klan and what happened to Al Smith (whatever it was that did happen to him).

All this might be possible. It certainly would be useful. I venture to say that today it is necessary. This period in American history is critical, not organic (to use Professor Toynbee's distinction). We face a crisis that is new in history. We would do well to face it with a new cleanliness of imagination, in the realization that internecine strife, beyond some inevitable human measure, is a luxury we can no longer afford. Serious issues confront us on all the three levels of public argument. Perhaps the time has come when we should endeavor to dissolve the structure of war that underlies the pluralistic society, and erect the more civilized structure of the dialogue. It would be no less sharply pluralistic, but rather more so, since the real pluralisms would be clarified out of their present confusion. And amid the pluralism a unity would be discernible—the unity of an orderly conversation. The pattern would not be that of ignorant armies clashing by night but of informed men locked together in argument in the full light of a new dialectical day. Thus we might present to a "candid world" the spectacle of a civil society.

ABOUT THE AUTHORS

GERHARD LENSKI is Professor of Sociology at the University of North Carolina. He was formerly on the faculty of the University of Michigan. In addition to *The Religious Factor*, he is co-author of *Principles of Sociology* and is currently working on a book to be titled *Power and Privilege*, which will be an attempt to develop a general theory of social stratification.

CLARK E. VINCENT is Chief of the Social Sciences Section in the training branch of the National Institute for Mental Health. He received his Ph.D. at the University of California at Berkeley where he later taught as a Professor of Family Sociology. Among his publications are: *Unmarried Mothers* and *Readings in Marriage Counseling*.

SEYMOUR MARTIN LIPSET is Professor of Sociology at the University of California at Berkeley. He is the author of *Political Man* and *Agrarian Socialism*, co-author of *Union Democracy* and *Social Mobility in Industrial Society*, editor of *Society in America*, co-editor of *Class Status and Power*, and of *Culture and Social Character*. His latest book on *America: The New Nation* is about to be published.

JAMES S. COLEMAN is Professor of Sociology in the Department of Social Relations at Johns Hopkins University. He received his Ph.D. at Columbia University. Later he taught at the University of Chicago. Among his publications are *Adolescent Society* and *Community Conflict*.

WILL HERBERG is Graduate Professor of Philosophy and Culture at Drew University. He received his Ph.D. from Columbia University. In addition to *Protestant-Catholic-Jew*, he has written *Judaism and Modern Man: An In-*

terpretation of Jewish Religion, and has edited *The Writings of Martin Buber, Four Existentialist Theologians* and *Community, State and Church: Three Essays k Karl Barth.*

JAROSLAV PELIKAN is Professor of Historical Theolog at the University of Chicago, where he received his Ph.D. He is the author of *The Cross for Every Day,* of *Evolution after Darwin,* and of *The Shape of Death,* and co-author of *From Luther to Kierkegaard.*

GUSTAVE WEIGEL is Professor of Ecclesiology at Woodstock College. He is a leading Jesuit theologian who served as dean of the theology faculty at the Catholic University of Chile until he was appointed to Woodstock College in 1949.

EMIL L. FACKENHEIM is Professor of Philosophy at the University of Toronto, where he received his Ph.D. He is an ordained rabbi and has written widely on theological and Judaic subjects.

SIDNEY HOOK is Professor of Philosophy at New York University, and has been Chairman of the Division of Philosophy at New York University's graduate school. He received his Ph.D. at Columbia University. He has been the author of many books including *From Hegel to Marx, The Hero in History, Paradoxes of Freedom, Political Power and Personal Freedom,* and *The Quest for Being.*

LEO PFEFFER is visiting Petegorsky Professor of Constitutional Law at Yeshiva University and General Counsel of the American Jewish Congress. He is the author of *Church, State and Freedom,* of *The Liberties of An American* and of *Creeds in Competition.* He has participated as counsel in almost every major church-state case that has come up through the American courts in the past fifteen years.

WILBER G. KATZ is Professor of Law at the University of Wisconsin Law School. He previously taught at the University of Chicago Law School for over thirty years, and served as dean of that law school for over ten of those years. He is Chairman of the Commission on Church-State Relations of the Protestant Episcopal Church.

JOHN COURTNEY MURRAY is Professor of Theology at Woodstock College. He was ordained a priest of the Society of Jesus in 1933. He has been the editor of *Theological Studies* and previously served as associate editor of *America*. He has also taught at Yale University. Among his publications is *We Hold These Truths*.

EARL RAAB is a staff consultant at the Survey Research Center at the University of California at Berkeley, and Associate Director of the Jewish Community Relations Council in San Francisco. He has written on, taught, and been actively engaged in the field of intergroup relations. He has served on the governing bodies of the National Community Relations Council and the National Association for Mental Health, and is an officer of the National Association of Jewish Community Relations Workers. He has taught at San Francisco State College and has lectured extensively. He is the author of *Major Social Problems* (with Gertrude Jaeger Selznick), among other works, and the editor of *American Race Relations Today*.

SOCIOLOGY